BART'S KING-SIZED

BOOK OF FUN

BART'S KING-SIZED

BOOK OF FUN

BART KING

Illustrations by Chris Sabatino

GIBBS SMITH
TO ENRICH AND INSPIRE HUMANKIND

Manufactured in Shenzhen, China in May 2010 by Toppan Printing

First Edition
14 13 12 11 10   5 4 3 2 1

Published by
Gibbs Smith
P.O. Box 667
Layton, Utah 84041
1.800.835.4993 orders
www.gibbs-smith.com

Printed and bound in China
Gibbs Smith books are printed on either recycled, 100% post-
consumer waste, FSC-certified papers or on paper produced from
a 100% certified sustainable forest/controlled wood source.

Library of Congress Cataloging-in-Publication Data

King, Bart, 1962-
  Bart's king-sized book of fun / Bart King ;
illustrations by Chris Sabatino. — 1st ed.
      p. cm.
  Includes bibliographical references.
  ISBN-13: 978-1-4236-0641-3
  ISBN-10: 1-4236-0641-8
  1. Amusements—Juvenile literature. 2. Creative activities and
seat work—Juvenile literature. I. Sabatino, Chris. II. Title.
  GV1203.K644 2010
  793—dc22
                          2010011438

TO MY SISTERS: GRETCHEN, KATHLEEN, MELINDA, SARAH, AND MARY. LOOK, YOU'RE ALL EQUALLY FUN, OKAY? (IT'S NOT A CONTEST!)

CONTENTS

INTRODUCTION

You have the right to have fun.

Y ou do not have to remain silent while you have fun. That would be sort of weird. Is it possible to have fun that way? I guess! Maybe if you read this book while stifling yourself, you could do it.

You have the right to talk to a parent before having fun, but this can sometimes reduce the amount of fun you have. If you do not wish to consult your parent, you can borrow mine for a moment. They will tell you to be careful and to go ahead and have fun.

Knowing and understanding your rights as I have explained them to you, are you now ready to have fun?

If your answer is yes, that's great. I've now accomplished a dream I've had since breakfast this morning!

FUN F.A.Q.S!

S ure, fun is a lot of fun, but how do you find it? In your quest for fun, it's possible that you might look for it in some of the wrong places. Heck, you might even face an un-fun situation! (See p. 295.)

Question: Is reading fun? Sometimes (like with a book like this) I wonder.
Answer: Why, you little scamp—

Whew! Okay, I'm calming down with some deep breaths. To explain whether reading is actually fun, I have to tell you a little story:

In 1900, a man named Joshua Slocum published a book called *Sailing Alone Around the World.* This true story described Slocum's three-year journey as he went sailing alone around the world. (You saw that coming, right?) Adults loved the adventure story, and so they made kids read it, too. In fact, a writer named Arthur Ransome thought that any young readers who DIDN'T like the book "ought to be drowned at once."

So looking at it that way, reading is fun. *Very* fun, thank you.

Question: I've had a lot of fun with my stuffed animals over the years. But now that I'm 12, maybe I'm a little old for them. What do you think?

Answer: This is a good question. Many of us feel we may have outgrown the things that once gave us so much fun when we were younger. Why do we feel this way? Are we afraid of being teased? I'm not sure.

But I can tell you that you are never too old to have a blankie or a stuffed dog, duck, or donkey. Isn't that right, Mr. Cuddles? You're a good widdle bear, aren't you? Yessums, I've had you for years and years, and you're the best widdle bear there is— *[Editor's Note: Let me interrupt this sad little speech to tell you that stuffed animals can be professionally dry-cleaned.]*

Question: I'd like to travel in time. Can I do it?

Answer: Sadly, no. But amazingly, it WAS once possible. A girl went back in time and saw her father in high school. He was wearing bell-bottom jeans and a gold chain. And his hair was permed!

This was so traumatic for the girl, time travel had to be outlawed.[1]

Question: Do people who smile a lot have more fun than others?

Answer: Yes. And not only do smiley people have more fun, but they may also be easier to be around than others! Here's what I mean: Researchers did a study of yearbook photos and found that the people who smiled in their pictures were more likely to be happily married later in life. (People who actually *frowned* in their photos were five times more likely to get a divorce than smiling people!)

Wow! Next, the researchers found there was a relationship between a person smiling in ANY photo (even ones taken of people when they were 10) and being happily married later in life!

Lesson: Have fun, say "cheese," and smile, smile, smile!

Question: Thank you for the *cough* useful tips. Anything else I need to know about fun?

Answer: Just this: Fun comes from creativity and enthusiasm. So if you *think* something is going to be fun, it probably will be!

1. But there is one loophole. If you ever change phone numbers, keep your old one. Wait one year, and then call it. When someone picks up, it will be the *old* you from yesteryear talking to the *new* you from right now!

But the bad news is that if you think something is going to STINK, it probably will. It's lucky for us that what makes life fun is your attitude . . . and you can always change your attitude![2]

Example: You're in a restaurant and you're starving. It's going to be a while before your food arrives. So you COULD sit there thinking about how you're ready to start chewing on that kid at the next table. Or you could let something fun distract you while you wait!

So you grab everyone's silverware and make a tic-tac-toe design on the table. Then you challenge your dad to a match using sugar packets and little jelly containers for the Xs and Os. By the time your food gets to the table, you'll have won enough jelly containers to be rich for life! (Okay, maybe not. But at least the time will pass more quickly!)

Question: Speaking of restaurants, is there a food that smells more "fun" than any other?
Answer: Good question! Nothing cheers me up like coming into the office first thing every morning and smelling the fried bologna that my employees cook up for me.

---

2. You can also change your socks. (I'm just saying.)

AWESOME ACTIVITIES

Dang, did you see that? Just now, right outside the window? That was the world going by! Don't ask me how something as big as the world can waltz around back and forth outside your window, but it's doing it right now.

You might be tempted to go check it out, but here's an even better idea. Just keep reading this cool chapter on activities. And if one of them sounds like fun, get up (*gasp!*) and try it.

Or you could just take a nap. (Because that's an activity, too!)

When you wake up, you might even have a new idea for your own activity. That's what happened to Walter Lines. In 1897, the fifteen-year-old woke up and then came up with a cool idea for a wheeled gizmo he could zoom around on. Walter told his father about the idea, but his dad was not impressed.

Walter had to wait a few years until he had his own toy factory. Its best-selling item was the invention he'd come up with as a boy: the scooter!

Using Walter as my inspiration, I have also invented a few things, including metal-detecting shoes, the umbrella tie, and the dog vacuum. But perhaps the finest invention I've ever seen is a combination of two things: music and video!

BIZARRE MUSIC VIDEO

For this activity, you need access to a friend and a baby.[1] Got 'em? Okay, now start quizzing that baby on where it keeps its clothes. Because you need one of the baby's onesies! (Or at least one of its shirts.)

Next, you need a video camera. It can be on a cell phone or something more complicated . . . like a camera on a really nice cell phone. While you're taking care of this, think about this question: What song do you like singing along to the most?

---

1. I guess your friend could BE the baby, but it's probably best if they're not one and the same. And when I say "best," I mean that it's not a very good sign if your friends are all babies. What can you talk about with a one-year-old? (Baby: "Diaper rash stinks." You: "The diaper's no picnic, either!")

Now get some nontoxic colored markers and head to the bathroom. You need to draw a face on your chin! To do this, imagine that the bottom of your chin is the TOP of your head. So you need eyes and a nose beneath your lower lip! (Extra credit for elements like hair and a moustache or beard.)

Once you have your upside-down chin face the way you want it, it's almost show time! Get your song cued up. Put on a turtleneck. Lie down on the ground. Have your camera operator get ready to film you upside down (so your chin's at the top of the frame). Oh, and that onesie? Pull it over your head and down to your upper lip! (The arms should be around your ears.)

And . . . action! Start the song, begin filming, and sing along or lip synch to the tune. When you're done, show the music video to the baby. I guarantee he'll either cry or be impressed!

MOVIE FUN!

If you're watching a movie at home, the first thing to come up on the screen will be the FBI Anti-Piracy warning. When this appears, say in a disappointed way, "Oh, I've seen this one already!" (This also works in theaters, but you have to say it when the Universal Studios or MGM icon comes up.)

BODY OUTLINES

The police don't actually put chalk outlines around the bodies of murder victims anymore, but we all know what it means if we see one. That's why you should surprise your neighbors by putting a chalk body outline on the sidewalk or road in front of where you live!

If you do this anytime in October, people will assume it's for Halloween. So don't do it in October! If you do it in November, you can make a chalk body outline of a turkey. December? Santa Claus! Easter? A bunny! Don't forget to draw the floppy ears!

Fun Tip: Have a ton of leftover Valentine's heart candies? They make pretty good sidewalk chalk!

ANTI-MONKEY BUTT POWDER?

Hey, did you know there's a product called Anti-Monkey Butt Powder? This information is so wonderful, I am just sitting here in amazement. Let's say it again: *Anti-Monkey Butt Powder.* Wow! It's intended to relieve the skin irritation that comes from too much sweating or chafing. (You know, like when you're on your tricycle seat for hours on a hot day?)

I haven't used Anti-Monkey Butt Powder before, but I like saying it almost as much as I like saying things like "ridonkulous" and "polyurethane foam." And since it's supposed to be good for you, I suggest sprinkling a bit of Anti-Monkey Butt Powder on things just to make life interesting.

At school: "Hey, I put some Anti-Monkey Butt Powder on your lunch bag."

While babysitting: "See how your sock monkey has a red butt? Let's put some Anti-Monkey Butt Powder on it to see if it gets better."

BUBBLES VARIETY PACK

As a child, I had a terrible allergy to bubbles. If I saw another kid blowing bubbles, I would break out in a rash! To keep me safe, my parents often put me in a protective box. They also called me the "Anti-Bubble Boy," which they found funny.

But now I've outgrown that childish allergy, and I can play with bubbles all I want. So let me present you with these cool bubbly activities!

PING-PONG BUBBLES

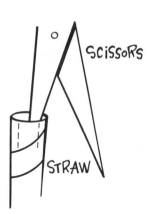

For this, you need a flexible drinking straw, a pair of scissors, and a Ping-Pong ball. With a pair of scissors, make five short cuts on the drinking end of the straw. Open and bend out the cuts so that you can set the Ping-Pong ball in there. Now blow! If you maintain the proper airflow, you can make the ball hover over the straw perfectly!

STRAW TOP

GROSS BUBBLES

Hey, while I'm thinking about bubbles, here's another activity! But I should tell you, it's really gross. In fact, it involves putting baby shampoo in your mouth. They say it's safe for a baby's eyes, so it should be safe for you, right? First, you should put on a baby bib, or at least a T-shirt that you don't like. Next, squirt some of the baby shampoo into your hand—but not too much! You don't want it dripping all over the place!

Bring your handful of shampoo up to your mouth. Now put it in! Yes, it tastes bad. But it's not THAT bad. Keep the shampoo at the FRONT of your mouth. *You don't want to swallow it!* (It's nontoxic, but still.) Open your mouth and blow gently outward. Bubbles! BIG bubbles!

CHALLENGE FUN!

Have someone sit in a chair and cross her legs with the right leg on top. Then have her move the end of her right foot in a clockwise direction. Finally, ask her to draw a "6" in the air with her right hand. As she does this, her foot will reverse direction![2]

2. *Cool Tip:* If you draw the "6" from the bottom up, you can do this without your foot changing direction.

TINY BUBBLES

If you have a brand-new flyswatter around the house, try this activity: Pour some bubble fluid into a Frisbee. Now dip the flyswatter into the bubble solution and then wave it around. LOTS of little bubbles will go flying!

BUBBLE IN A BUBBLE

Get a drinking straw and a regular container of bubble fluid with a wand. Dip half of the straw into the bubble fluid. Then dip the wand and softly blow a bubble out of it. Now catch the bubble on the wand! With the bubble balanced on the wand, poke the wet end of the straw directly into the middle of the bubble. Blow softly into the end of the straw. *Ta-dah!*

GIANT BUBBLE CRAZINESS

Fill something big with bubble solution, like a kiddie pool or a gigantic dog dish. Now dip a hula hoop into it! With your fingers on the outside edges of the hula hoop, raise the hoop out of the water and move it through the air. If you're careful, a huge bubble will appear!

★ No hula hoop? Try running a piece of string through two drinking straws. Run the string long enough so that you can make a square with two straw sides and two string sides. Tie off the string. Then make the square by holding the straws and dip it into your bubble solution!

WHEN BLOWING THINGS UP WASN'T FUN!

The first toy balloons came out in the early 1800s. But you had to make them yourself using a container of liquid rubber and a syringe. After filling the syringe with rubber, you pushed down its plunger and out came your balloon! But you couldn't touch the balloon, as it had to dry first. (After all that work, you'd be mad if someone popped your balloon!)

THE ANIMALS ON THE HILL

This activity is fun to do with young people and those who like animals. Arrange two chairs so that one person can sit across from you. Ask the person to relax, and then gently reach out and hold the person's left wrist with your left hand. Because you want the person to trust you, you should be very slow with your movements!

Say to the person, "See if you can guess what animal is climbing up your arm." Then with your right hand, use your fingers to start crawling up his left arm.

The person will probably say something like "a spider" or "a bug."

"Good!" you answer. "Now, what's this?" Turn your right hand sideways so that the edge of your palm is on the person's arm. Then slide your palm back and forth up the person's arm.

The person will probably guess "a snake." Again, give him praise.

Do one more where you take your right hand and make little jumps up the person's right arm. (Any guess like a kangaroo, a rabbit, or a flea is fine.) The whole time, you're being very positive and trustworthy.

Finally, say, "Can you guess why all these animals are climbing up your arm?" As the person considers this question, make a fist and bang it all the way up his arm.

Your subject will recoil in surprise and look at you in shock! And that's when you say, "Because a big elephant is coming after them!"

SEE CALENDAR FOR EVENTS!

Each year, the people of Telluride, Colorado, celebrate their Nothing Festival. Its motto is "Thank you for not participating." Some of the festival's events include:

★ Sunrises and sunsets occur as normal.

★ The force of gravity continues to be in effect.

★ A sense of humor search happens daily.

BODY LANGUAGE, PART I

The non-verbal way for someone to show he's got his eye on you is with the following hand gesture:

1. He makes eye contact with you and makes a "V" symbol with his forefinger and middle finger.

2. He points his two fingers at his two eyes.

3. He turns his hand around and points his two fingers at you. You've been warned!

There are a number of fun ways to alter this silent message. For starters, try making eye contact with someone. Make your "V" symbol, and then when you point your two fingers at your eyes, pretend to have poked yourself in the eyes!

This is always funny, though it's less convincing if you wear glasses or if you have two glass eyes.

If you suspect someone has "let one" (or if YOU have let one and you want to avoid blame):

1. Make your "V" sign.

2. Point to your two nostrils and grimace.

3. Point to your suspect accusingly.

BODY LANGUAGE, PART II

For this, you're going to need an iPod or cell phone that can shoot video. Got one? Good.

Practice moving your nose around. You know, try to sneer with one nostril, and then both. Practice scrunching up your nose. Work on dilating your nostrils. Once your nose is warmed up, shoot an up-close video of your entire routine for thirty to forty seconds.

Now hold up the iPod in the middle of your face (the iPod should be covering your nose and facing out) and hit play. Your video nose will start hamming it up while the rest of your face plays it cool!

If you want to get tricky with this method, get two iPods. Shoot a short video of someone else's eye on each of the iPods. As with your nose, the eyes should be rolling around, winking, opening wide, narrowing, etc. When you're done, cover YOUR two eyes with the two iPods and roll 'em!

As the two eyes rotate around onscreen, try making long, drawn-out sounds: *"Wooowee wowow bleeooorg!"* (For some reason, this helps.) Little kids will especially enjoy this.

If someone in your audience doesn't like your awesome act, do this:

1. Make a "V" sign with your two fingers.

2. Use your fingers to remove the complainer's pancreas.

PLAYING WITH KIDS!.

Kids love make-believe structures like forts made by draping a blanket and pillows over a table. (But kids get upset by make-believe nuclear attacks that turn the table over and scatter the pillows.)

WATER MAGIC

S harpen some pencils. Get them really sharp! Now get a small plastic bag and bring it and the pencils over to the sink. Fill the bag about 3/4 full with water. Now tie a knot in the top. Okay, you're ready!

Take one of the pencils and spear the bag with it! Do this quickly, so that the pencil goes in straight and then pokes through the other side of the bag. You'll be surprised to see that if you poke the pencil through the bag fast enough, no water will spill out of the bag!

If you have the knack for this, poke more pencils into the bag. It's pretty impressive what a pincushion for pencils a bag full of water can turn into . . . without leaking!

MESSAGE FUN!

Give yourself a new voicemail message. Or better yet, get your hands on someone else's cell phone or answering machine and give him or her a new message! A couple of ideas:

1. "We're sorry, but you have reached an imaginary number. Please rotate your phone 90 degrees and try again."

2. "This is KFRC, and you're on the air!"

THE STRAW THAT BROKE THE . . . STRAW'S BACK?

The first time I saw this trick, it actually sort of scared me. That's because the person showing me the trick popped his straw so loud that it sounded like a firecracker. The fact that he did it in a restaurant just made it that much more . . . fun. (So thanks for that, Troy.)

Grip a drinking straw firmly at both ends. You want to grab it so that no air can get out of its 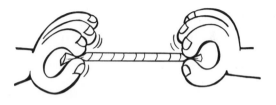 ends. Then start rolling it up from both ends. (If that's too hard, just wind up one end of the straw a couple of times, and then start rolling down the other end.)

 Winding the straw will get more difficult as you roll to the middle. That's because the air is all compressed in there! When you can't take it anymore, have someone flick the straw (it should now look like an air bubble) hard with their finger. If they do it right, the straw will explode! (Don't worry, there's no danger—but it can be loud!)

THE POWER OF ADVERTISING!

In 1913, a guy named Charles Pujeau came up with Tinker Toys. Nobody cared. So to advertise them, Pujeau hired some little people, dressed them up as elves, and had them play with Tinker Toys in a store window. The next year, Pujeau sold a million sets!

THE INVISIBLE FIRE EXTINGUISHER

Do this in the kitchen! Get a candle and light it.

Now get a large measuring cup. The best kind would be one with a pour spout on the side. Pour some white vinegar into the measuring cup. Not too much! Pour just enough vinegar to cover the bottom of the measuring cup, and then add a little bit more.

Now put a spoonful of baking soda into the vinegar. As you know, this will make the vinegar get really fizzy! The resulting bubbles will release carbon dioxide. What's cool is that carbon dioxide is heavier than regular air, so cover the bubbling solution with your hand or a newspaper or something else. This will keep the carbon dioxide inside the measuring cup.

Once the bubbling dies down, carefully lift the measuring cup. Hold the cup over the lit candle and "pour" out the carbon dioxide onto the candle. As the carbon dioxide drops down, it will push any oxygen around the candle out of the way and put out the flame!

PUNKIN FUN!

For some real high-tech fun, get some pumpkin seeds! But don't get just ANY pumpkin seeds. Make sure yours are for the Atlantic giant pumpkin. These gourds grow anywhere from 40 to 800 pounds! If you want your giant pumpkin in time for Halloween, plant it 115 days before October 31. (That means the seeds should be in the ground by July!)

MAKING WATER DISAPPEAR!

This activity can ONLY be done in the kitchen or another uncarpeted indoor area. (You'll see why in a moment.)

First, you need a broom or broom handle (mops also work), a stepladder (if you're short, make that a full-size ladder), and a large plastic bowl. If the plastic bowl has a "dimple" in the middle of its bottom, that will be helpful, but it's not necessary.

This trick won't work unless there's an unsuspecting person in the house with you. If there is, do this: Set the stepladder in the middle of the floor. Then pour water into the plastic bowl until it's about 2/3 full. Grab your broom handle and the bowl and move to the stepladder.

Carefully climb the stepladder until you can reach out and press the bowl up against the kitchen ceiling. When you can, take the end of the broomstick and push it up on the center of the bowl. As you push against the bowl with the stick, you can let go of it with your hand. Then carefully step down the stepladder so that you're standing on the floor with the bowl held against the ceiling above your head.

Now call your "volunteer" into the kitchen. Tell him to hurry—you have an awesome magic trick to show him. As he comes in, quickly say, "Okay, hold this stick! I'm going to make this bowl disappear!" He may be confused, so just act excited, like what's going to happen is the coolest thing ever . . . but he needs to come hold the stick!

Once you're sure the person is holding the stick with enough pressure to keep the bowl up, step back, grab the stepladder, and run out of the kitchen. Your volunteer will most likely be thinking, "Hey, this isn't right." If so, he might let go of the stick . . . and the bowl will come down!

If the person DOESN'T let go of the stick, it might be interesting to see how long he'll hold onto it. Or you could run into the kitchen and poke, prod, or tickle him to try to make him drop the bowl. But however you look at it, that bowl of water WILL come down!

DEAD JUICE SOLDIERS

If you drink as many juice boxes as I do, you probably have some empties lying around right now. (I call them "dead juice soldiers.") Take the straw from one of those boxes and tie a knot in the end of it. Now shove the straw about halfway into the box, with the knot sticking out.

Now aim the straw end of the box away from you and anyone else. Stamp on the box really hard with your foot! (You could also hit it with a mallet.) Watch that straw fly!

It turns out that dead soldiers CAN still shoot!

ACCENTS ARE FUN!

Did you know that learning foreign languages is good for your brain? It is, really. Also, knowing a second language helps open the world up to you. For example, you can finally understand what those people at the airport are talking about. (Hey, they like your shoes!)

But if you don't have time to learn a foreign language right now, just work on picking up a foreign ACCENT. You're better at this than you might think. You see, when you were just a little creature inside the womb, you could hear your mom's voice whenever she spoke. (Seriously.) And after you were born, you cried with whatever accent your mom had. (I'm still serious.) Yep, French babies cry with a French accent, German babies cry with a German accent, and you cry with, uh, your own particular accent. (In fact, you're probably crying in that accent right now!)

You are custom-made to pick up on the accents you hear. So, what kind of accent do you want? Just like learning a foreign language, the best way to learn an accent is to listen to a native speaker. Failing that, you can look elsewhere. For example, you could listen to the BBC News for an English accent, or you could watch Indonesian cartoons for an Indonesian one.

What's the world's best accent? Everyone has an opinion, but the right answer is "Italian." Okay, and what's the world's worst accent? Again, it's a matter of taste. A Dutch person might find a Chinese accent annoying. And a Chinese person might dislike a Zimbabwean accent. But I think ALL people can agree that a BabyTalk accent is the worst:

"Oh, look at widdle baby's gweat big eyes and his widdle-widdle toesies . . . Oh, did you dwop your toy? I'm sowwy!"

Blech! Now go forth and speak in accents in peace.

THE MOST EXCITING LOTTERY OF ALL! (GLOVES NOT INCLUDED)

Before I describe this, let me ask you a question: Do you only give out presents on birthdays?

If your answer is yes, I'm going to ask you to change your mind. You can give presents *anytime*. Especially cheap, funny presents! Here's what I mean. I was just in a shop called the Monkey King (cool name, huh?), and I saw a small sumo wrestler figure. The little wrestler was weaving back and forth because it was solar-powered.

Do you understand? It was a *solar-powered sumo wrestler.* (I know. It's so cool, I can't breathe right now!)

I just had to get the sumo guy, but I didn't know who to give it to. So I stuck the sumo guy in a box and taped it shut. Then I took that box and put it in a slightly bigger box. Then I put that box in a bigger box. And then I did it one more time, so that the sumo wrestler was in FOUR boxes!

Then I got a pair of big leather gardening gloves out of the garage. Ha! I was ready!

Finally, I invited three people over to my house. I picked up the box and explained that it contained a priceless gift. (This was sort of a lie—the sumo wrestler was cheap!) Then

I explained that each person would be wearing the gloves for twenty seconds. During that time, they were to try to unwrap the fabulous package. Whoever actually opened the package got to keep the gift.

To see who gets to go first, pick the person whose last name comes last in the alphabet, and then start the timer. You'll be amazed at how much fun this is. The laughter and excitement will make every dollar you've spent (all two of them!) well worth the investment.

MIXED MARTIAL AIR ARTS!

If you and a friend are just sitting around killing time AND if you both have long sleeves on, try this. Pull your arms in from their sleeves and hold them behind your back. Then start twisting your body at the hip (sort of like playing with a hula hoop) so that your shirtsleeves swing out and around. Once you and your friend get your sleeves swinging, it will look like the craziest fake fight of all time! (Extra Fun Points if either of you gets knocked out.)

A DEEP QUESTION

H ey, do people still go bobbing for apples? If you haven't tried it before, bobbing IS fun. But it's also a little weird to stick your face in a tub of water that some other kid was just drooling in!

If you find yourself bobbing for an apple (or any other fruit or vegetable), here's how to win. Pick out an apple. Get your face positioned over it. Open your mouth wide and take a deep breath. Now bend your face down to the apple. As you do this, the apple will try to escape by diving below you. So keep pushing your head underwater until you get to the bottom of the tub/barrel. When the apple hits the bottom, bite into it and bring it to the top!

Depending on how deep the water is, you may be drenched, but who cares: you're a champion bobber!

For a less wet version of this game, put a bunch of whipped cream, slushy ice cream, or gravy into a giant bowl. Then set a small apple (or some other fruit) on top of it and let people start bobbing. (And the winner gets to take home the gravy in a zip-lock bag!)

BLINDFOLDED FUN!

Write the names of unusual items (toilet, pickle, cactus) on strips of paper and put the strips of paper in a baseball cap. Have a person seated with a piece of paper and a pencil pull out one of the strips. He should read the strip but NOT show anyone what it says. Then have him close his eyes and start to draw. As he does so, the rest of the group tries to guess what it's a picture of!

MAKE A SEAT, TAKE A SEAT

I used to show students how to do this in my homeroom. I had to stop when someone spilled apple juice everywhere. (It was horrible!)

Anyway, this activity is totally safe. First, you need four people who are all about the same size. You'll also need one extra person who is any size at all.

Arrange four chairs so that they form a square, facing inward. The corners should not quite touch. Then have the four people sit in the chairs. Their legs should be sticking out on the left side of their chair, not the front. All set?

Each person should now lean back so that their shoulders and the back of their head ends up on the legs of the person to their right. Once the people have all done this, they should brace themselves . . . because the fifth person is going to come around and slowly remove all the chairs!

If everyone digs in, you will now have a human table!

STAPLER FUN!

To do this activity, you need access to two pretty high-tech items: a stapler and a piece of paper. Now try stapling your name into the paper. This is surprisingly tough. (It's also the most fun I've had since that time I *almost* went to Disneyland!)

THE RING FINGER TRICK!

Did you know that it's impossible for most people to lift their ring finger from certain positions?

So let's try a trick! First, spread your hand out flat on a table, with your palm facing the table. Ask another person to do the same thing. Have the  person imitate you as you raise and then lower each of your fingers individually, as shown above.

Now take out a dollar bill. Raise your hand and turn it, palm out, toward the other person. Bend down your middle finger. Have your subject hold his hand the same way. Then press your hands together, as shown below.

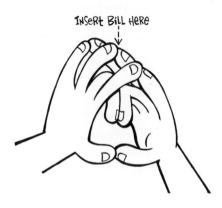

INSERT BILL HERE

Slip the dollar bill between the two ring fingers. Tell your subject he can have the dollar if he can lift his ring finger away from yours so that the dollar falls down to the table. (No cheating by just pulling the whole arm back or moving the finger to the side!) The faces the person will make are going to be priceless, so you may want to have a photographer handy for this event.

(By the way, if the person CAN do this without cheating, he or she has superpowers and has earned the dollar!)

COMMON FLY; UNCOMMON SUPERPOWERS!

The next time a fly gets loose in your house, keep an eye on it. After the fly lands on the ceiling, it prepares to do something pretty amazing: to dismount, the fly grabs the ceiling with its front legs, and then it does a reverse somersault. Then it starts flying around!

SHADOW POWER!

For centuries, wizards have utilized the magical power of shadows. I have no idea why; my shadow has never done anything for me. (And that's why I had it surgically removed!)

And now prepare yourself for the most needless instruction in this entire book: To make these shadows, you'll need a light source, like a lamp or flashlight. (You're welcome!)

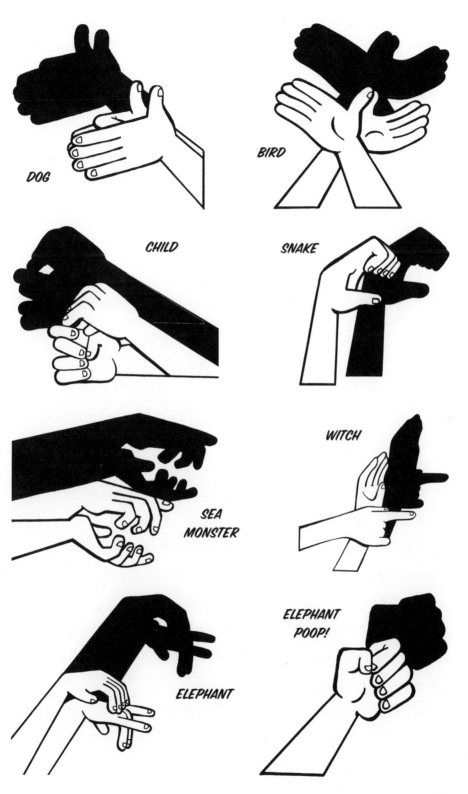

DOG

BIRD

CHILD

SNAKE

SEA MONSTER

WITCH

ELEPHANT

ELEPHANT POOP!

THE DRAMATIC UNDERWEAR MOVE

Let me write this slowly, so that the words sink in:

Quickly pulling out your underwear (in one piece!) is the most dramatic gesture you will ever make in your life.

Hmmm, I typed that slowly, but I still read it at regular speed. Oh, well!

Anyway, the idea is that sometime soon, you will be very happy. Maybe you will have just hit a winning Ping-Pong shot. Or perhaps you just blew out all your birthday candles on your first try. *Yes!* Or maybe you turned your homework in on time. That's ... great.

Anyway, at moments like these, you can try to high-five someone else, or maybe do a fist pump. But why not reach back and pull your underwear out of your pants? (Actually, there are a number of reasons not to do this. Ignore them all!)

There is a slow and complicated way to pull your underwear out of your pants in one piece, but no one's going to wait around for you to do that. So instead, get dressed like usual, but wear an untucked shirt or blouse. This will allow you to carefully fold an EXTRA pair of underwear in the back of your pants! When your big moment comes, you can:

1. Reach back with an intense expression.

2. Make a grimacing face as you pretend you're ripping loose your underwear.

3. Hoist your underwear in victory as people applaud!

Note: Remember to use clean underwear for this trick, or there won't be very much celebration.

BACK WHEN DINOSAURS ROAMED THE LAND . . . AND MEN CARRIED PURSES!

You know what's fun to have? Pockets! I mean, think about it: without pockets, where would you put your lint? Before the 1600s, hardly anyone had pockets. They hadn't been invented yet! If you wanted to carry something, you held it in your hands, tucked it into your hat, or carried a (*gasp!*) purse!

Bonus Weirdness: The first pockets that were invented hung on the OUTSIDE of people's pants.

MISCHIEVOUS FUN

You're in the elevator. A person is running toward you, shouting, "Hold the door!" But you freeze up! And as the person approaches, the door shuts just before he reaches it. Poor guy! Hey, wait a minute . . . did you just *smile* as the door closed?

Yes, you were slightly entertained by the small, painless injustice that just happened to that person. The Germans have a special word for this feeling: *Schadenfreude* (SHAW-den-froy-duh), which means "joy from another person's misfortune."

While Schadenfreude is *normal*, it is also a *false* joy. Should you feel guilty about it? Probably! But let your conscience be your guide. If you see someone slip on a banana peel, put the clamps on your Schadenfreude and see what you can do to help. And if you see someone getting embarrassed, try to help un-embarrass him!

It is only under two important conditions that you can enjoy Schadenfreude:

The "He Was Asking for It" Rule: Have you ever seen a person being naughty, and then, almost by magic, he suddenly "gets what's coming to him"? Once, I was being a jerk and stole a piece of Halloween candy from my sister. Mean, I know. But hey, I was only seventeen. I didn't know any better!

As I ran off chuckling, I looked back over my shoulder and stubbed my toe against a wall. Falling to the floor, I rolled in pain while my sister calmly came forward and confiscated her Bit o' Honey.

"Serves you right," she said. Wow! She got to enjoy her candy AND her Schadenfreude!

And just last month, I was out riding my bicycle when I came to a stop sign. A guy pulled up alongside me on his motorcycle and looked over at me with a sneer. He revved his engine like he wanted to race, or perhaps say, "Listen to that motor!" Then, with a squeal of tires, he was off. But he had to steer around a traffic circle, and as he did this, he turned his tire too much, wobbled, hit the curb, and catapulted onto someone else's front lawn!

As he sat up in confusion, a pedestrian asked if he was okay. He said "yes" and started looking for his motorcycle.

And as I pedaled slowly past and waved, he just looked at me and shook his head.

It was the greatest moment of my life! (So thanks, Schadenfreude!)

FAMILY FUN!

If you're out with your family and someone *asks* if you're out with your family, say, "No, I met these people on the Internet." Oh, the laughter! This line also works if you're with your family and you see someone *you* know but your family doesn't. (When your parents ask how you know the person, you say, "I met him on the Internet.")

The "Nobody Got Hurt" Rule: Your dad is changing a baby boy's diaper. As the diaper comes off, the boy pees. The stream of urine hits your dad on his shirt and face.

After crying out in alarm, your dad wipes himself off, gets the dirty diaper off, and gets a new one on. Then he lifts up the baby and holds him on his shoulder, where the baby promptly throws up. Setting the baby back down, your dad wipes off the baby barf and then sniffs the air.

"What's that?" he asks suspiciously.

"Smells like Junior pooped his pants again," you say helpfully.

It is now okay to laugh at the expression on your dad's face.

Now, to test your understanding of when Schadenfreude is appropriate, let's take a test. Imagine the following:

1. Your sister just got a diary. Not a blank book, but one of those diaries that has a glossy cover and comes with a cheap lock.

"Don't let me catch you trying to read this!" she warns you.

Sheesh, you weren't even interested in it—until now! So the next time your sister is gone, take a paper clip. Unbend it a little and then find her diary. Stick the clip into the book's lock . . . and *leave*!

That's right, just leave! You see, that way, when she finds the paper clip and confronts you, you can honestly say that you DIDN'T read her diary!

Are your actions acceptable?

A. No, because you are intentionally winding your sister up. Uncool.

B. Yes, because she asked for it and nobody got hurt. Cool![1]

2. You cut the power to a building that has automatic doors. (Based on the movies I watch, this is easy to do.) Then you watch and chuckle as people walk into the glass doors.

Are your actions acceptable?

A. No, because someone might smash his nose or spill a latte.

B. Yes, because this is so funny, it bypasses all rules.[2]

Now you can explore the world of fun at the slight expense of someone else. Remember, this person MUST be someone whom you know well, like a relative or a good friend. And he or she can't be younger or smaller than you are and must have a good sense of humor. Okay? Let's get started!

FLIP-FLOP!

For this, you need a coffee mug. You also need some wax paper or a plastic sheet that is *not* sticky.

1. These are *both* good answers!
2. It's unlikely anyone would hurt themselves walking into a glass door. But cutting the building's power could give *you* a mild electric shock!

Fill the cup almost all the way with water. (Another liquid would also work, but water is easiest to clean up.) Now go to a large surface (like a table) that doesn't have any precious laptops or papers on it. Cover the top of the cup with the wax paper. Pull the paper taut around the edges and hold your hand over it. (Just to be safe, you might even want to wrap a rubber band around the mouth of the cup to hold the paper in place.)

Now quickly flip the cup over so that it's upside down! I know this sounds impossible. It isn't. Keeping pressure on the cup, the next step is to quickly pull the paper or plastic sheet away from the bottom of the cup. Got it? You now have a full cup that is upside down on the table.

You probably spilled a little bit in the process, and that's normal. Clean up the spillage, and now let the cup sit, because sooner or later, someone's going to pick it up and freak out!

Bonus Cup Trick! Go online and find a picture of a pig's snout. Print and cut out the picture, and then tape it to the bottom of a coffee cup. And try not to laugh when someone drinks and looks like a pig!

KETCHUP-FILLED DOUGHNUT

I f you're ever around some jelly-filled doughnuts . . . and you have a straw . . . and a squeezable bottle of ketchup . . . then try this! Take the straw and shove one end into the doughnut's jelly hole. Then suck out the jelly!

Leave the straw where it is. Use a towel to wipe off the end you were sucking on, and then shove that end into the little opening in the ketchup bottle. You'll find that when you squeeze the bottle, ketchup goes INTO the doughnut! Oh, happy day!

Stop squeezing when the doughnut is full again. Then leave it for someone to enjoy.

HOMEMADE STINKINESS

O kay, check the cupboards to see if there's any valerian root powder in the house. If not, you can get it in the herbs or supplements section of your local market. (In a pinch, valerian tea can also work.)

Valerian root has been used since ancient times as a remedy for things like insomnia. What's especially interesting about it is that it sort of smells like ripe cheese. And that's why I'm speaking to you today! Get some valerian root powder (by breaking open some capsules or a tea bag) and put a couple teaspoons in a small jar that you can shut tight. Before you shut it tight, add a couple teaspoons of vinegar!

Now QUICKLY close the jar and start shaking it. Okay, here's the key: once you open that jar, it's going to stink like crazy! (In a nontoxic, organic, friendly stinky way.) So you'll probably want to get away from the jar after you open it and put it under someone's bed or in someone's closet.

There are two other interesting things about valerian root. First, even though it stinks, cats seem to like it! And second, *because* it stinks, people once believed that elves and other magical creatures hated it. (In Sweden, it was apparently not unusual to put valerian root on a groom's clothes to keep away jealous elves on his wedding day!)

HOKEY-POKEY FUN!

If you know someone who has an "In" and "Out" tray on her desk, add a third tray that says, "Shake It All About."

It's possible that in all the give-and-take of your mischief, your friend may ask you, "Now are we even?"

To this, feel free to respond:

A. "I guess. Now I can't *even* look at you."

B. "If you mean do I want to get *even* more revenge upon you, the answer is yes."

PEN-ITENTIARY!

You know how some pens have plastic "plugs" in the non-writing end? If you have *two* of these pens, pop out the end plug of pen #1. (It's easy.) Then remove the cap from pen #2 and pull out the ballpoint and ink. In the now-empty end of pen #2, stick the plug from pen #1. Pen #2 is now a two-plug pen! Now put the cap back on pen #2. The next time somebody uncaps it, he or she will be totally befuddled!

KNOW-IT-ALL FUN!

B eing a know-it-all has to be pretty fun. Why else would there be so many know-it-alls in the world? Especially since experience has taught me that:

Nobody likes a know-it-all!

So why would anyone want to *be* a know-it-all? It can be very satisfying (in a smug way) to sit there thinking that YOU have the answer. In fact, one thing I really like is when there's a quiz show on television and I know the answer to the questions. (Yes, I'm as smart as a fifth grader!) I have even more fun when the contestant doesn't know the answers. (This is not good, I know.) That's why I liked hearing these actual questions on the quiz show called *The Weakest Link*:

Host: What kind of dozen is 13?
Contestant: Half a dozen.
Nope. It's a "baker's dozen." I knew that! Here's another good one:

Host: What was Hitler's first name?
Contestant: *Heil.*
No! It was Adolf. Man, I'm a genius! I could win a fortune if I just went on one of these programs. I told my niece this one time when we were watching. But she wasn't impressed after this happened:

Host: What was the principal language used by the ancient Romans?
Contestant: Greek.
Me: *Ha!* That's the silliest answer ever!

My niece: Actually, it was very common for Romans to learn Greek. It was a sign of education.

Me: This is not fun any more.

But even though my know-it-all balloon got popped, I learned an important lesson. Sometimes when you think the other person doesn't know what he is talking about, it just might be YOU who doesn't know what you're talking about.

(But at least a baker's dozen is still 13!)

FUN LATIN PHRASES

Latin rules! Or at least, Latin *used* to rule, back in the days when it was the official language of the ancient Roman Empire. And from that mighty position, Latin helped create later languages like English, Spanish, and Klingon.[3]

There are lots of good reasons to learn Latin phrases. After all, there are hundreds of thousands of Latin roots in English, and the legal system is full of Latin phrases. And these Latin words are super-easy to learn. For example, do you know the Latin word for *"Ouch!"*? It's *"Uah!"*

See what I mean?

3. Oops. *Not* Klingon!

But the best reason to know some Latin is so you can show off. That's because Latin is the ONE great exception to the rule that nobody likes a know-it-all. Here are just a few examples:

Tene simian meam. Hold my pet monkey.

Imago brachium amisit—triste est. It's too bad that statue lost his arm.

Licetne mihi in fabis pendere? Can I pay in beans?

Habesne ludos tabulae ullos bonos? Have you got any good board games?

Remove hunc puerum; clamosissimus est. Take this child away; it's too noisy.

Cave canem. Beware of the dog.

Iuva me! Nuper ab minivan transcursus sum. Help! A minivan ran me over.

Suntne scabies tuae meliores? Are your scabs better yet?

Odor horribilis! That stinks!

Di immortales! @&$%!

Crocidili liberi sunt! The crocodiles have gotten loose!

WHAT DO THEY HAVE AGAINST KINGS?

The ancient Romans rid themselves of their last king in 510 BCE. After that, one of the worst insults you could give any Roman was to call him or her "king" or "queen"!

INCREDIBLE INVENTIONS
& Creative Costumes

When a person gets a good idea for an invention, the smart thing to do is to *trademark* it. That means the idea is officially registered with the government . . . and THAT means nobody else can steal it!

Let's say you're riding in a car. Looking around, you notice there are airbags stored all over the place. "Hmmm," you think. "If airbags can be hidden inside a car, couldn't they also be hidden inside someone's pants?"

You start imagining a pair of pants equipped with airbags! If the person wearing your airbag pants ever started to fall down or otherwise get in an accident, his pants would fill with gas![1] And this is how your idea for Airbag Pants is born!

Soon, you're drawing up plans for your Airbag Pants. Of course, you have to decide what parts of the pants should inflate. Knees? Yes. The butt? Of course! The ankle cuffs? *Please!* When was the last time someone wiped out on a skateboard and staggered around yelling, "My ANNNKKKLLE!"

Once you're done with your design, you take it to the US Patent and Trademark Office. An official looks your Airbag Pants over and then gives you a thumb's up.

"These would go great with the Airbag Undershorts!" the official says.

1. Yes, some people are capable of filling their pants with gas without any help.

"What?!" you cry. And you learn that just a few days earlier, three guys trademarked the idea of Airbag Undershorts. But that's okay! People who want to be super-protected could wear both!

GNDN EXPLAINED!

Set designers for science-fiction shows have to create real-looking technology that doesn't do anything at all. So the set designers for the original *Star Trek* series labeled many pipes and tubes with the letters "GNDN". It was an in-joke that stood for "Goes Nowhere, Does Nothing"!

BATHROOM STEREO

Have you ever been taking a shower, and all of a sudden you wish that you could listen to some good music while you're taking care of business?

Me too!

Luckily, you can make your own bathroom stereo. All you need is a big drinking glass and a small digital device (like a Smartphone) that plays music. Here's what you do: Set the glass on a hard surface like a counter, away from towels and water. Then turn on your cell phone's music and set the phone in the glass!

Make sure the phone is "speaker-side down." By getting the speaker close to the bottom of the glass, the music will then bounce up and out of the glass with surprisingly good quality!

HAVING A DISCO BALL!

I know, it's sad. You WANT to dance in your room, but without a disco ball, you just can't get in the mood. Well, despair no longer! Try cutting up an old CD into small squares and triangles. Then loop some string around a craft ball (or any old ball you have bouncing around). Finally, glue the CD bits to the ball and hang it!

REMOTE-CONTROL PUMPKIN

 et's say you have a remote-control car. Ready? You and I have to say it together at the same time:

"You have a remote-control car."

Here's a thought. What if you were to put something on top of the car to camouflage it? I just tried putting a wig on mine, so that it would look like some hairy creature scuttling around. But the darn hairs keep getting wrapped up in the axles!

Ah, but what about a small pumpkin? This could be perfect for spooking trick-or-treaters on Halloween!

First, take off the outer shell of your remote-control car to get an idea of how big it really is. Now take it with you when you go to get a pumpkin! Your pumpkin should just fit over the car.

When you get home, carve out a hole in the BOTTOM of the pumpkin. Remove the guts and then compare the car to the pumpkin bottom. Just notch away the parts of the pumpkin that might get in the way of the car rolling around.

And if your pumpkin works well, attach a sweeping device to the front so that it can clear your porch of leaves and candy wrappers the day after Halloween!

DIY PARADE FLOAT RACE!

The city of Ferndale, California, hosts a yearly race with the coolest slogan ever: "Adults having fun so children want to get older." That's the idea behind the Kinetic Grand Championship, a race in which contestants invent, make, and then ride on wacky human-powered vehicles that must cross over forty miles of road, sand, and water. The vehicles (or "kinetic sculptures") all have moving parts—like flapping wings and blinking eyes—so they look like demented parade floats. Some of the event's super-fun awards include the Golden Dinosaur (for the first sculpture that breaks down), the Golden Flipper (for the best wipeout), and the prized Mediocre Award.

COSTUMES

A wise woman once said, "Ask a little kid what he wants to do and he will shrug. But if you tuck a pillowcase into his shirt and tell him it's a cape, suddenly he's a superhero."

Ain't that the truth! Of course, costumes are fun for kids of all ages. And they can be so simple! For instance, someone in my family (hi, Dad!) likes to pull up his pants as high as they will go and then walk around as if there were nothing unusual about it. And my brother-in-law takes any excuse to waltz around in a kilt. And he's *Irish!* But dressing in costumes is good for the imagination, so if my brother-in-law wants to pretend he's Scottish, fine. (Did I mention he's Irish?)

So what do you want to dress up as? Or are you helping a younger kid get an idea? The younger a child is, the more fun it is for her to pretend to be older. So let a young one dress up in adult clothes, like maybe a pantsuit. This also works in the other direction. That is, *you* can pretend to be younger by dressing like a toddler. Just wrap yourself up in a blankie and start sucking your thumb like mad. If you want to get more realistic, find some oversize diapers. (But *please* remember your potty training.)

If you decide to dress up as a really old person, here's a trick: scrunch up your face and put on some makeup that's lighter than your usual skin tone. Now un-scrunch your face. Using an eyeliner pencil (brown is best), color in all the spots where your natural wrinkles are. Be sure to draw crow's feet around your eyes and add lines down the sides of your nose. Finally, add a bit of baby powder to your whole face, and put a bunch of it in your hair to make it look gray!

If you want to look YOUNGER than you are, just do all this in reverse.

Before you put on a costume for a full day of school or trick-or-treating, think about this stuff:

★ How comfortable is your costume?

★ Can you go to the bathroom while wearing it?

★ If you're going to be walking around at night, how well can you see through your mask?

★ If you're going to be running from zombies or authority figures, how fast can you move? And what if the zombies ARE authority figures? ("*Principal McGee, noooo!*")

Okay, here are some cool costume ideas. If your name is Karen, I have some good news: This first costume idea I got from a girl named Karen! You see, one Halloween, Karen wore a brown plastic garbage bag over her body. She also had on dark glasses. (She didn't have a white cane, but that wouldn't have hurt.)

Me: I don't get it.
Karen: I'm a blind date!
Me: I get it.
Thanks, Karen! Here are a few other ideas:

Piñata: What if you found a cardboard box big enough to walk around in? You could turn it upside down and cut a hole in the bottom for your head. Add a hole to two sides for your arms, and you're ready to add details! Piñatas are decorated with colored fringes of paper glued to a hollow container . . . like your box! So cut some strips of newspaper and make your glue with a mix of two cups of water to one cup of flour. You can either dip your newspaper strips in the glue or lay the strips on the box and then brush on the glue. To add shapes to your piñata, use blown-up balloons, crumpled paper, and other pieces of cardboard. Need to make arms? Roll up some newspapers. Need another head? Stuff wads of paper into a paper bag.

When you're done, let the glue dry for a couple of days, and then paint the box and/or add kooky trinkets. You'll be looking good! Of course, the downside to being a piñata is that someone might take a swing at you with a stick. To avoid this, hand out your own candy—and carry your *own* stick!

Alien: In my experience, aliens have antennae and green or blue skin. Oh, and also, you might want to wear a metallic outfit. Try to find clothing colored like silver, gold, or unobtainium.

Chewed Gum: Wear a pink outfit and then find a doll table and stick that on your head. (Or just strap a shoe to your noggin!)

H-E-Double-Hockey-Sticks Angel: Make a halo with rolled foil or a wire hanger (or a wire hanger covered with foil!). Now put on a leather jacket. If you look tough in a heavenly sort of way, you're done.

Deviled Egg: Get an egg costume. Then put on horns! But don't add a forked tail. (Eggs don't have tails, silly.)

Leaf Blower: Get a big leaf. Hang it from the bill of a baseball cap and put the cap on your head. When asked what you are, blow on the leaf. *Ta-dah!* (Hey, where did everyone go?)

Greek God: Drape yourself with a white sheet. Next, cut out a lightning-bolt shape from a cardboard box. Cover it with foil and start smiting mortals. ("Release the Kraken!")

Shooting Star: Get a big cardboard box. Next, cut out two giant stars from the box. These two stars should be at least big enough to cover your body from the waist up. (Once you cut out the first star, you can just trace around it to make the second one.) 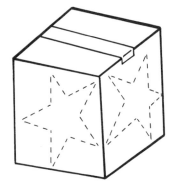 Now you that you have two big stars, you're going to wear them over your shoulders like a sandwich board. To do this, use a hole punch to make holes in the cardboard. Then reinforce the holes on the INSIDE

sides with duct tape or those paper reinforcement things that stationery stores sell. Then run some string between the holes in the two stars so that you can wear them over your shoulders! Finally, get a colorful plastic gun to wave around, and you're all set!

Macaroni and Cheese: Get one of those big cheese hats like Green Bay Packers fans wear. Then stick macaroni noodles all over your clothes.

The Undead: For some reason, zombies don't seem to wear new clothes, so the older and more ripped up your clothing, the better. Also, zombies are dead. (Who knew?) So you should probably get some light-colored makeup for your face and hands. After putting down a white/light base, add some green highlights for the spots where fungus is growing. Sweet!

Of course, fake blood is always a nice touch.[2] It might just be me, but I always think that a little blood trickling out of the eyes is ghoulishly cool. (Or "coolishly ghoul"?) And get some blood around your mouth, too. For another cool effect, dip a brush or comb in your fake blood and then drag it across your skin. Don't forget to apply dark eyeliner to give you that "serious" zombie look.

For ambitious zombie costume makers, try making an exposed bone. Your best bet is to cut off a piece of a white candle at an angle. Stick it to yourself with some liquid latex and finish it off with some fake blood.

Really, Really Gross: For hanging intestines, get some old panty hose. Use a pair of scissors to cut off the legs. Then get someone with mad sewing-machine skills. (A glue gun could also work.) You

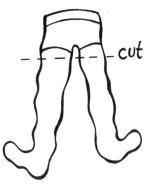

want to get a seam going down the *middle* of each

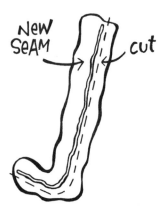

of the two legs. Once you've done this, take the scissors and cut along the seam on either side. Now you have two thinner panty hose legs! Turn the legs inside out and stuff them with fabric,

2. To make fake blood, take one cup of corn syrup and add ten drops of red food coloring and one drop of green food coloring. Stir and apply!

cotton, and cloth scraps. As you do this, periodically give them a twist or two and use a glue gun or safety pin to hold the twist in place. This helps the panty hose look like intestines! Finally, put on an old button-down shirt and snake the panty

hose in and out of the holes in the front (or any extra tears in the shirt fabric). And for your final touch, it's best to soak all of this in fake blood!

FACIAL HAIR?!

We have now entered the most important part of this book: understanding that facial hair is fun! In order to explain this, first let me ask: Have you ever seen a man with muttonchops? A guy with a goatee? Some dudes with Fu Manchus?

Well, it turns out that all these people have a GREAT sense of humor!

I mean, they *have* to . . . otherwise, they're growing weird beards because they think it looks GOOD. But that's *impossible*. Therefore, men with facial hair *must* have black belts in fun.

And that's why boys, girls, and all other types of humans should take every chance they get to have facial hair, too! You can buy your own facial-hair kit from a costume shop or make your own with cotton balls, felt, or the pelt of some small mammal. But what KIND of fake hair will you grow?

Perhaps the silliest (and therefore the most fun!) type of facial hair is the *sideburn*. These used to be called side-whiskers or muttonchops, but the famous Civil War leader General Ambrose Burnside (1824–1881) changed all that. Burnside's side-whiskers were so huge (they connected with his mustache), he got the honor of having sideburns named after him! (They were called *burnsides* first, and then sideburns later on.)

Today, we still call beefy sideburns *muttonchops*. Muttonchops with big bottoms are "Wolverine" style. And

sideburns that start down the face and then rise above the upper lip to join the mustache are known as either the *Franz Joseph* or *"friendly muttonchops."*

Now, have you ever seen a mustache combined with a chin beard? I call that a pudding ring! But most people call it a

goatee. It turns out that most people are wrong; a goatee is just a small pointed beard, like a goat has. (No mustache!)

If the goatee is just on the bottom of the person's chin, it's called a *poet's beard*. If there's only a wee bit of hair below the bottom lip, it's a *soul patch*.[3] And a soul patch that grows down and joins with a chin beard is called an *anchor!* A narrow, pointed chin beard extending from the chin is an *impériale* (or "royale"). And finally, a chin beard like the *impériale* combined with a waxed mustache is a *Van Dyke*.

Before moving on to beards, let me just check to see if there's more than one kind of mustache. *checks notes* Uh-oh. There is!

Stashburns: Sideburns that come out and become one with the mustache!

Pencil: The least-fun mustache, because it's so thin, you barely notice it. (Never trust someone with a pencil mustache.)

3. Chuck Klosterman once wrote, "In the 10,000 year history of facial hair, no one has ever looked nonidiotic with a soul patch." (Klosterman has a full beard.)

Dalí: Waxed up like a cartoon mustache.

Handlebar: This is a healthy mustache that swings up at the ends, like the horns of a steer.

Chevron: A thick mustache that covers the whole upper lip but stops short of going into the mouth.

Hungarian: A Chevron on steroids! Huge bristles sticking out like a walrus.

Pancho Villa: A thick, droopy mustache.

Horseshoe: Another droopy 'stache, but this one is squared off at the top, like a horseshoe. (It's popular in movie Westerns.)

Fu Manchu: The coolest mustache! It droops like a Pancho Villa, but it goes all the way below the chin!

And now, the beards! A *stubble beard* is just one to four days of growth. This barely beard became popular in the 1980s, and is still with us today. Yay. The next-most-simple kind of beard is the *chinstrap beard*. It's just a narrow beard that

follows a line along the jaw and chin, but it has no mustache. If you see one, it's probably pretty short. Why?

Well, there is only ONE thing worse than a long chinstrap beard. And that's a long *neck beard.* (I've seen one, and I've been trying to un-see it ever since!) The best-looking version of a chinstrap beard is the *Lincoln beard.* It can be long and full, and it should cover most of the chin.

A friendly looking beard is the *Verdi.* This is a round, short beard with a big mustache—sort of what Santa Claus would have if he got his beard cut back. And then there is the *full beard,* which is what I call any healthy, bushy beard that provides a natural environment for small forest animals!

Protecting the natural beauty of full beards is the business of heroic groups like the Beard Liberation Front. This group organized a protest against the film *Harry Potter and the Chamber of Secrets* because it had actors (like the guy playing Hagrid) who were obviously wearing *fake* beards. The horror!

HOBBIES

I just realized that the way most people "make" fun is with their hobbies. And right here in this gigantic dictionary that's crushing my legs it says a hobby is "an activity done regularly for pleasure."

That means reading can be a hobby. That's right, reading is an *activity,* since it actually engages your brain. You can't just stare at a book and get anything out of it. You have to read, think about, and interpret the book instead. Hobby!

Hmmm, so is listening to music a hobby? I say yes, especially if you *really* listen to it. After all, it just might make you get up and shake your booty!

Now, I don't want to criticize anybody's hobbies, but if someone's main interest in life is watching TV, he could do better. A LOT better. (Since when is sitting and staring an activity?) Here's a better idea: Go on a scavenger hunt! These are *almost* always fun.[4] One good version is the "bigger and better" scavenger hunt. This works best if you have a neighborhood of friendly people. Each team starts with a time limit and an item that's pretty lame (like a paper clip or a broken pencil). Then they start looking for an item that is bigger and/or better than what they have. If the

4. The first one I ever did, I misunderstood how they worked and brought home a raccoon, a buzzard, and a coyote.

team can find such an item (either by asking neighbors or keeping their eyes open), they trade their current item for the new one. The winning team is the one with the biggest, best item within the time limit!

If this doesn't sound that great to you, here are some other hobby possibilities:

★ Fish
★ Teach a fish to fish
★ Learn a language
★ Learn to teach a fish a language
★ Garden
★ Garden a fish (wait, this isn't working!)
★ Walk
★ Travel
★ Collect pencils
★ Socialize (NOT online!)
★ Go to a coin shop (this is surprisingly fun)
★ Ride a bike
★ Volunteer
★ Play cards
★ Hike
★ Join a Mustard-of-the-Month Club
★ Collect air-sickness bags
★ Take photos of yourself using your air-sickness bags
★ Camp
★ Snowboard/ski
★ Collect wrapping paper
★ Hang out with animals
★ Go bowling
★ Learn a new dance
★ Go to see a play
★ Put on your own play
★ Shoot pool
★ Go to the beach
★ Sing Estonian show tunes

In the country of Estonia, the most popular hobby is singing in a choir. This makes sense to me. It can be pretty fun to sing in a choir. First, you get to sing really loud and no one yells at you. Instead, people yell WITH you . . . in harmony! And second, there's nothing like that feeling of being part of a larger group, a group that has one voice, together, building to one great note! (This must be especially fun if you're singing in Estonian.)

THERE'S NO BUSINESS LIKE SNOW BUSINESS!

According to the American Hobby Association, "folding and cutting paper" is the third-most-popular hobby among kids. That means the odds are pretty high you've done the project where you make a snowflake out of paper.

But be warned! An expert on ice formation named Professor Thomas Koop recently complained that many paper snowflakes don't have six points. In nature, almost every snowflake is "hexagonal" in this way.

So if you accidentally cut out a snowflake that has eight points, it is a "fake flake" and must be DESTROYED IMMEDIATELY!

WILD WORDS

You may think it's impossible for words to be fun. But since "fun" IS a word, I disagree!

If you think that's the weakest argument of all time, you might be right. So let me quickly move on to say that *good* writers can arrange words so well, their work practically becomes a form of art.

You can do this, too! For example, try combining two words to form a *new* word. It's perfectly legal! Let's say you're trying to wipe a kid's face after a meal, but he's squirming and wiggling around too much. So you say, "*Stop *squirmling!"* He'll be so impressed, you'll get the rest of that stew off his face without a hitch.[1]

By being creative, people can come up with marvelous new words and phrases. But other times they say things that are just plain dopey! Here are a couple of my favorites:

In 2009, a convicted bank robber named Trammel Bledsoe was waiting for the judge to sentence him when he said, "Can you hurry this up? I don't have time for this."

Judge Lawrence F. Stengel answered, "You'll have all the time in the world." Then he gave Bledsoe forty-one years in prison.

1. *Squirmle* and other word combinations are called "portmanteau" words.

And politician Barbara Boxer once declared, "Those who survived the San Francisco earthquake said, 'Thank goodness I'm still alive.' But of course, those who died, their lives will never be the same again."

Hmmm, clearly, words can get you into trouble. In fact, some words are so troublesome, you shouldn't even THINK them. You know what words I'm talking about! Words like (dare I write it?) "*meep.*"

Yes, *meep!* "Meep" became a bad word when the kids at a school in Massachusetts started using it one day. Of course, there's nothing really wrong with meep. It's just an innocent word from the *Muppet Show* that doesn't mean anything at all. But if a whole lot of students start meeping, you can see how there wouldn't be much learning. So the school banned "meep"!

This actually made "meep" seem like a tough word from the bad part of town. But because of reverse psychology, many people who had always ignored "meep" then started using it. Popular ways to use meep now include:

★ An expression of happiness. (Example: You get up and the sun is shining. *"Meep!"*)

★ A greeting. (Example: You greet the sun. *"Meep!"*)

★ An expression of surprise. (Example: The sun goes supernova and explodes. *"Meep!"*)

This is so cool! Hey, I just read about how scientists can combine the cells of a goat and a sheep so that they grow into an animal called—wait for it—the *geep!*

In addition to naming new animal species, words can also be handy tools for getting at the truth. Heck, if someone says something that you agree with, a decent slang response is "Word."

Parent: This *Fun* book was a questionable purchase.
You: Word.

But for some reason, many people insist on using words in a way that *confuses* the truth! This happens to your parents when they go to work. They get messages like these all the time:

★ "This project is so important, we can't let things that are more important interfere with it."

★ "What we need is a list of specific unknown problems we will encounter."

★ "We know that communication is a problem, but we're not going to discuss that now."

To help avoid confusion, you know what would be a good idea? If we had an *international* language! That way, people of all nations could understand each other and the world would be a better place. I'm not the first person to think of this. In the 1920s, a group called the League of Nations recommended the same thing! They even had a language picked out. It was called *Esperanto*, and it was an easy-to-learn combination of Spanish, French, English, Greek, and other European languages.

All the League of Nations members agreed except for one: France! At the time, French was thought of as the international language. And France fought so hard against Esperanto, everyone kind of gave up on it.

And so the world never got around to communicating. (Thanks, France!)

Today, we're stuck with hundreds of different languages. Heck, even when you think you're speaking English, an American can go to England and be misunderstood. That happened to me. I was in a London bookstore when I hit my elbow on a shelf. As I grabbed my elbow in pain, the bookstore owner asked if I was all right. And when I answered, I forgot that the word "bum" means "butt" in England!

"Yeah," I said, "it's just that I have a bum elbow."

First, the bookstore owner looked at my elbow.

Then she started to glance down at my backside, but caught herself. So she just gave me a look of confused concern.

Anyway, since I already went to the trouble of writing this book in English, let's talk about it. English is definitely a quirky, fun-loving language! One unusual thing about English is that it includes words from all over the world. Here are a few of my favorites!

bowerbird: A person who collects useless objects.

crambazzled: A word that describes someone who looks older than he is.

deipnosophist: A person who's fun to talk to.

fornale: Spending money before you have it.

mulligrub: Depression.

nudnik: An annoying, boring person.

onomatomania: Anger at not being able to find the right word.

petrichor: The nice smell that comes with the first rain.

shot clog: An annoying friend whom you put up with because he or she buys you stuff.

stridewallop: A tall, awkward woman.

twack: A shopper who asks a lot of questions but never buys anything.

It was in the United States that one of the coolest words of all time was invented: *puckerstopple* (to be embarrassed). Sadly, this word is not used much anymore, which is a great source of puckerstopplement for me. Other awesome words made in the USA include:

goshbustified: Very pleased.

glomp: To jump and hug someone from behind.

sockdologer: A heavy blow.

blustrification: Celebrating loudly.

dumfungle: To use up.

absquatulate: To leave quickly.

GROUP NOUNS ROCK!

One hippopotamus is called a *hippopotamus. Duh!* But what is a *bunch* of hippopotamuses (or hippopotami) called? A "bloat."

Knowing this will come in handy the next time you're riding your bike to school and you need to say, *"Look! A bloat of hippopotami!"*

There are lots of other group nouns that are interesting—like these!

★ A flange of baboons.
★ A rhumba of rattlesnakes.
★ A business of ferrets.
★ A scourge of mosquitos.
★ A knot of toads.
★ A mob of emus.
★ An unkindness of ravens.

A MOB OF EMUS

But sometimes it might be better just to *invent* a cool group name for something. For example, a bunch of butterflies is usually called a swarm. But that makes them sound like grasshoppers! I think that "a rainbow of butterflies" is much better. And I'm not even sure what it *should* be, but I've decided to use "a plateful of platypuses" the next time I see more than one platypus. It's only a matter of time!

A gentleman named David Malki! (that's how he spells it) came up with the following labels for more unusual creatures:

- ★ A lawn of gnomes.
- ★ A dignity of dragons.
- ★ A snarl of minotaurs.
- ★ A lunacy of werewolves.
- ★ A flurry of yeti.
- ★ A basement of vampires.
- ★ A vexation of zombies.
- ★ A clamor of clones.
- ★ A jake of Jedi.
- ★ A tournament of Predators.
- ★ A clangor of robots.
- ★ A torment of ogres.
- ★ A malevolence of trolls.
- ★ A cackle of mad scientists.[2]

2. Adapted from the Stoakes-Whibley Natural Index of Supernatural Collective Nouns: http://wondermark.com/566.

SOMEONE TELL ME WHAT THE MEEP IS GOING ON!

As everyone knows, "#$%@&!" is a bad word. To learn more about this, ask an informed adult or hamster why "number sign/dollar sign/percent/ampersand/and/exclamation point" is so horrible. (And then explain it to me!)

THIS IS ME!

When it comes to answering the phone, "Hello?" is not a fun word to use. I mean, that's what EVERYBODY says. And if life has taught me anything, it's that if everyone else is doing something, it's probably not as fun as it could be. (The only exceptions to this are blinking, eating ice cream, and wearing black socks.)

As you know, Alexander Graham Bell (the inventor of the phone) thought people should say, "Ahoy!" when answering the phone. Too bad that idea didn't stick. If it had, we'd have "Ahoy Kitty!" lunch boxes and pencil cases everywhere! (My, that is droll.)

Phone Fun: When my brother answers the phone, he sort of draws out his first word so that it sounds like "YEL-low?" (I then say, "Orange!" but my brother has never found that funny.)

But it's not like early phone users started using "Hello" right away. In fact, picking up the phone and saying "Hello" was considered rude, and even vulgar! (Seriously.) But it turned out to be so handy, you can travel to almost any country on the planet today and answer the phone with a "Hello" and it will work.

How can we escape from the horrible tyranny of "Hello"? Back in the old days, the British answered this way: "Are you there?" (Of course, you were likely not to have a connection back then.) Some other possibilities are:

★ "This is Bart." Note: This only works if your name is Bart.

★ "Good-bye." This will totally blow your caller's mind, especially if you then hang up!

★ "Go." Wow! In one syllable, you just stated that you're there and the other person should start talking. ("Speak" could also work, but people might think you're talking to a dog!)

★ "nuqneH?" This is Klingon for "What do you want?" It gets right to the point, which is especially fun if you're a Klingon.

FUNNY-SOUNDING WORDS!

A television program called *The Goon Show* identified *lurgy, needle nardle noo, ploogie,* and *plinge* as some of the funniest words ever. (They're all made up.)

FUN NICKNAMES!

I like almost all nicknames. I also like learning how people get them. For example, some people have "sound effect" nicknames. In fact, I have a sister who got her nickname because as a toddler, she often climbed out of her bed and fell to the floor.

Boom.

No worries. She was okay.

But what really sealed the deal was the time Boom fell down the stairs.

Boom, boom, boom, boom, boom, boom, boom, boom, boom, boom, boom, boom.

Boom was still okay! In fact, I cried more than she did when this happened. (I'm very sensitive.)

A great way to get a creative nickname is to let someone from another country give you one. For example, the Chinese nickname for basketball player Carlos Boozer is Betrayal Skull Dude. Wow! And Chinese crowds cheer wildly for Kobe Bryant, aka the Little Flying Warrior. (But maybe something's being lost in the translation, because Kobe isn't little!) The Chinese gave a less flattering nickname to bicyclist Jeannie Longo Ciprelli. Since she has competed in seven different Olympic Games, Ciprelli is affectionately known to the Chinese as "Grandma."

Not cool!

Getting back to my sister, Boom is a pretty cool nickname. In fact, I've been thinking about it, and almost ANY nickname that isn't totally insulting is pretty awesome. However, there is a boy nickname I would skip: *Skip*. The problem with "Skip" is that it's just a small jump to "Skippy"! And no human should ever be called the same thing as peanut butter. (So I guess "Chunky" is a bad nickname, too.)

Maybe I have such a high tolerance for nicknames because my real name is "Bart." What a rip-off! But things could have been worse. In fact, here is the story behind the worst nickname of all time:

The great artist Michelangelo finished his masterpiece *The Last Judgment* in 1541. It was awesome! A classic! Incredible!

But even so, some people had a problem with the painting. You see, *The Last Judgment* was a big painting with lots of people . . . and over three dozen of the men shown in the masterpiece were *naked*. Yikes! So another artist was picked to paint underwear. Lots and lots of underwear.

The lucky person picked for the job was Danela da Volterra. But he is better known today for his nickname, *Il Braghettone*: The Underwear Man.

This is incredible. Now I can talk about underwear AND nicknames! Did you know that underwear didn't even get invented until the 1800s? Before that, people left skid marks everywhere. *Ugh.* Though underwear today goes by names like "skivvies" or "tightie whities," its first nicknames included "unmentionables" and even "unwhisperables."

That's right, you couldn't even *whisper* about your underwear!

We have a healthier attitude about underwear these days. Not only do people say the word out loud, but the Australians have come up with a rich variety of nicknames for underwear Down Under!

* Acca Daccas
* Bog Catchers
* Boggle Pants
* Boodundies
* Bum Baggers
* Bumberdaks
* Dag Catchers
* Dakes
* Dakkers
* Duds Fundies
* Foundation Wear
* Fun Daks
* Fundies
* Geeto Bobblies
* Under-the-Butt Nut Hut
* Grundies
* The Incubators
* Jean Savers
* John Brumbies
* Mooshies
* Mr. Happy Pants
* Ninnies
* Scruds
* Scruts Jokies
* Scungies
* Skid Pans
* Skidy Scrapers
* Snag Slingers
* Tightie Whities
* Underdacks

Wow, that's such a great list, I hate to play favorites. But even so, I'm going to call my unmentionables "Bumberdaks" for the rest of the year!

CREATIVE WRITING

Writing is one of the greatest things you can do! (I read that somewhere.) In fact, perhaps the only bad thing about writing is that it can take so darned long to do. I mean, who has time to sit down and type out a book? Not me!

But you know what IS fun? Getting mail! I mean, getting real mail from an actual person. I got a postcard from my nephew the other day. On the front was a turtle. On the back my nephew had written, "I like turtles." That's it! And it was awesome.

SPELL CHECK FUN!

On your computer, type up a list of the names of your friends, and then run a spell check. Be amused at the new names the spell check creates! For example, on my computer, Stanley Tucci becomes "Stainless Taco." And Leonard Nimoy becomes "Leotard Gnome"!

In fact, I should send him a message back. Not an IM, not a text message, not a VM, not a tweet, not e-mail. Maybe I'll send him a postcard. (NO, not an e-card!) Yeah, and on the back I'll put a cool turtle joke (see p. 161). Because that's how I crawl—er, roll.

Of course, you don't have to write using snail mail. Do you keep a diary or a personal journal? Maybe it's just for yourself, or maybe it's for one of your classes. Either way, let's say that you're not sure what to put in it. Let me give you a Professional Writing Tip: If you're stuck, try writing a bunch of stuff that uses the word "I" a lot.

You're welcome!

If your journal is for a class, it's a good idea to add creative touches that your teacher will enjoy. Also, be sure to use as many emoticons and verticons as possible. (Teachers understand that these are terrific ways to express yourself.)

NOT-VERY-HANDY EMOTICONS

:X	Your secret is safe with me
;X	My lips are sealed (but I crossed my fingers!)
=L	Drooling
|-O	Yawning
:-\	Uneasy
~(8(l)	Homer Simpson
qo{-<]:	Kid on a skateboard

SQUIRREL STRENGTHS!

The longest English word of one syllable is "squirreled." And the longest English word with only one vowel is "strengths."

AMAZINGLY USELESS VERTICONS!

\,,/(^_^)\,,/	Rock on!
\(^o^)/	Excited!
(-_\\\\)	Feeling emo
(9ò_ó)=@	Throwing a punch
(9ò_ó)=o=|:::⟩	Swinging a sword
(⟩”⟩) ˜)))’⟩	Chasing an armadillo
/\ *\o/*__	A shark attacking a cheerleader
@(*o*)@	A koala bear
‘~~)_)~~´	A roll of toilet paper
(,,,)=^¡^=(,,,)	A sleeping cat
(__(__)	A butt
(,,,)^@¡@^(,,,)	A cat that saw a butt that needs some toilet paper

THE SINCERO-MARK!

Did you know there's a company that has invented a new punctuation mark? It's called the "SarcMark," because you're supposed to use it when you're being sarcastic. (For legal reasons, I can't show it to you, but it looks like a backward ampersand (@).

The problem with the SarcMark is that I know some people who are ALWAYS sarcastic. So if they were writing a message, the thing would have a rash of SarcMarks all over it! For people like this, I have an emoticon that can be used for sincerity. It's this little guy giving two thumbs up!

continued on next page

continued from previous page

b(^_^)d

Just *looking* at this emoticon makes me smile! I call it the Sincero-Mark, and you should use it when you are writing something heartfelt, like *Happy Birthday, Mom!* **b(^_^)d**

If you want to give your Sincero-Mark just a little irony, try this version:

b(~_^)d

Ha! See? The emoticon is giving a knowing wink to give your writing the perfect tone! I'll bet you really love this book now! **b(~_^)d**

ENGLISH EXTRA CREDIT

Hey, why not write a hundred-word story that doesn't use the letters Z or X? (This will be easier than you think.) Then turn it in to your English teacher for extra credit! If your teacher doesn't understand, point to your paper's heading.

Then turn in your paper.

Your teacher's puzzled look probably means that your creativity amazes her!

If a hundred words seem like a lot, don't despair. In this age of Twitter,

MY ENGLISH 101 TERM PAPER:

"A VERY SPECIAL STORY THAT DOESN'T USE THE LETTERS Z OR X!"

by ALEX ZIPPERTON

you can just sum up a whole story in one sentence! For example:

★ After finding out her grandfather was in the army, my daughter asked, "Was he with the green guys or the tan guys?"

★ I have three giant bruises and a bruised ego as proof that you can, in fact, forget how to ride a bicycle.

★ After I circled B for the tenth straight time, I had to wonder if I was getting all the answers wrong or if my teacher just had a sick sense of humor.

What's that? I have a hard time believing that you're saying, *"I'll never have time to write a whole sentence!"* But in case this is true, try writing a *six-word* memoir. A "memoir" is your life story (or part of your life story).

Here's an example of a six-word memoir that a "friend" of mine wrote:

★ "Ate fast. Wrote books. Went bald."

And here are a few examples by teenagers from SMITH magazine:

★ "I never got my Hogwarts letter." Deanna H.

★ "I fulfilled my awkwardness quota today." Maggie A.

★ "My tenth toenail finally grew back." Blue L.

Speaking of writing, today I learned that there is a book titled *Soft Drink and Fruit Juice Problems Solved*.

Did you see that? There's a book out there that can solve your juice problems!

Just knowing that *Soft Drink and Fruit Juice Problems Solved* exists made me very happy. And so I wanted to do something nice for the authors. I decided the best thing I could do was write a review that might help others realize what a classic their book is.

Of course, I hadn't actually READ *Soft Drink and Fruit Juice Problems Solved*, but so what? The book had already improved my life, and a little review was the least I could do as repayment. So I went to a popular shopping Web site and wrote a five-star review:

This book is a valuable tool for anyone having juice and soft drink problems. Speaking for myself, I often have trouble spilling my fruit juice while walking to the monorail. While sippy cups have been helpful, it wasn't until I read Soft Drink and Fruit Juice Problems Solved *that I could make it to work without blueberry stains on my tie. Bravo to the authors!*

Writing that was so fun. Another good thing about silly online reviews is that others can join in with the good times! For example, maybe you've heard of the Three Wolf Moon T-shirt? This black shirt with three howling wolves and one full moon on it really cracked people up. It has almost two thousand reviews at one Web site alone, and many of them are *very* silly. But happily, almost everyone gives the T-shirt five stars, because it is NOT fun (or cool) to write a negative review of a silly product.

Other odd products, like ballpoint pens and wool socks, have also been flooded by funny reviews over the years. Of these, my favorite is the gallon container of Tuscan whole milk. It has over a thousand reviews—and they don't even make the stuff anymore! And as J. Fitzsimmons's review shows us, you don't have to write much to impress people: "Has anyone else tried pouring this stuff over dry cereal? A-W-E-S-O-M-E!"

Now got out there and write some awesome reviews for fun stuff . . . and remember, being positive is A-W-E-S-O-M-E!

NOT-SO-CREATIVE WRITING?

You can probably tell that I love to read. After all, there are a lot of great books out there!

The following is not one of them.

In 2009, rapper Kanye West co-wrote a book titled *Thank You And You're Welcome*. The book was fifty-two pages long, but some of the pages were blank! The pages that weren't blank had sentences like "Life is 5% what happens and 95% how you react!" (That quote covered two pages in the book, by the way.)

Why write a book that was so short? Kanye West explained in an interview: "I am not a fan of books. I would never want a book's autograph. I am a proud non-reader of books."

Well, I totally disagree with him about one thing: I think it would be awesome to get a book's autograph!

PHOTO MAGIC

Okay, you're getting ready to take a picture of your friend. But if your friend tries to look cool or serious for the photo, it's not going to be much fun. You need goofiness! Or at least a smile.

So before you snap the shot, you say something that photographers have used for millions of years to get people to grin. Yes, I'm talking about "cheese." Or am I? It turns out that not everyone relies on cheese for a good photo. Here are a few of the magic words that international photographers use:

China: *qie ze* (eggplant)
Denmark: *appelsin* (orange)

Finland: *muikki* (a type of fish)

Korea: *kimch'i* (pickled cabbage)

Poland: *dzem* (marmalade)

Spain: *patata* (potato)

Sweden: *omelett* (omelet)

Brazil: *sheez* (the letter "x")

Another fun thing to do is to take a picture so zany that it would make even the most jaded math teacher crack a smile. Ooh, I just had a good idea! Use one of your PARENTS' cameras for some of the following pictures. Then when your mom or dad looks through the shots later on, they'll be stunned at the insanity you've unleashed!

MONEYFACING

For this, you need paper money that has a human face somewhere on it. Let's imagine you're using a US dollar bill. You need one person to take the picture and one person to pose for it. The picture taker will fold the dollar bill so that the top half of George Washington's face is visible. Then she'll hold the dollar bill up in front of her subject's face. Finally, she'll position the dollar bill so that it fits the size of the real person's head.

The result is a hybrid known as a moneyface!

For variety, you can match the upper part of the real person's face with the lower part of the dollar bill . . . or perch the money's full head shot over your subject's shoulders!

And remember, for contrast, the more different the money portrait is from the real subject, the better. So try putting Abraham Lincoln's head on top of a baby. (All you need for this shot is a $5 bill and a baby!)

DAUGHTER/SON OF THE MONTH

Have you ever gone into a business that has pictures of its "Employee of the Month"? I love those pictures. And you can join in the fun!

First, snap a picture of yourself. Like an employee of the month, you should be standing proudly dressed in your typical outfit. (School clothes complete with backpack? A dirty coverall?)

Now get a cheap frame from around the house or from a shop that sells cheap frames. (If you're spending more than five bucks, it's not cheap enough!) I'm guessing it would be too much trouble to get your hands on a cool engraved bronze label that says "Son [or Daughter] of the Month," so just create and print out your own label when you print out your photo.

Frame your picture carefully (remember, as son/daughter of the month, you have to set an example). Then mount the picture in a prominent spot in your house and see how long it takes people to notice it!

FUNNY IN A WAY I CAN'T EXPLAIN!

This is funny. Don't ask me why. Take a picture (especially a small framed one) someone has up in their house and hide it in an odd place. This could be in the person's underwear drawer, next to their jumbo-size jar of peanut butter, or just behind another picture. Oh, the merriment!

BABY SHOTS!

For some reason, including a baby in a picture always makes it better. When my sister gave birth to identical twins, I thought it would be a great idea to give them matching outfits. One outfit would say "Copy" on the front, and the other outfit would say "Paste." Then we would take their picture![1]

Another great idea (that might be in bad taste) is this: Get a big frying pan and set it on the stove. (Make sure all burners and the oven are off, of course!) Put a soft blanket on top of the pan. Set up whatever vegetables and spices you have in the house near the frying pan. Now, gently take a baby and set it on the frying pan. Take a picture! (Bonus points if you can get a hungry-looking toddler to stand near the pan with a spatula.)

Or how about this? Take a bunch of dolls and line them up on a bed or sofa. And right in the middle of the doll lineup, stick a *real* baby. ("Say '*muikki!*'")

Finally, with the help of an adult, take a baby and go somewhere where there's a basketball hoop. Kneel down near the basket while holding the camera and aim the camera up in the air. Have the adult take the baby and (carefully!) put one hand on its tummy. Now have the person

---

1. Apparently, I was the only one who thought this was funny.

hold up the baby with one arm while looking at the basket. Start taking pictures! (It will look like the person was shooting baskets with the baby!)

GIVE YOUR DOG MORE HAIR

F irst, I just want to say that it's ALWAYS fun to dress up pets. One of the best pictures I've ever seen showed a pit bull wearing a big pair of rabbit ears. So funny. (It was the only Velveteen Rabbit I've ever seen that could bite your face off!)

Anyway, for this photo, you need a person with fairly long hair. This could be a girl or a hair-metal guitarist, but whoever it is, the more hair, the better.

Oh, and you also need a dog, the less hyper the better!

Have your dog sit in front of the camera. Now have the long-haired person sit behind the dog and lean forward so that his or her face is behind the dog's head. Now ask them to sweep all that hair forward! Adjust the bangs and give it a part. Now have Fido say, "Cheesy!"

Note: Be careful if you ever put a wig on your dog. The wrong wig can make it look like the dog has a mullet . . . and dogs hate mullets! (Scientists believe that millions of years ago, dogs used to hunt mullets in the wild.)

THE LYING DOWN GAME

T his is a favorite because it's so easy. Take a picture of yourself or a friend lying down in an unlikely spot. Examples might include a teacher's desk, a busy sidewalk, or a helipad!

MONKEY MANIA

T o do this photo project, you need to find all the stuffed monkeys you can get your hands on. If you can't get your hands on more than a few monkeys, go after other animals that might be found in a tree, like stuffed parrots, stuffed cats, and, uh, stuffed butterflies.

Once you have a collection of eight or more stuffed tree animals, find a tree. The tree could be in a park or at your house. Maybe it's in the front yard or outside your best friend's window. Now climb the tree and/or get a ladder and start putting the animals up in the tree branches! If you have trouble making the animals stay put, wrap their legs around a branch and then use a rubber band to keep the paws together. Once you have the animals just like you want them, take a picture. Better yet, see if you can lie in wait and get a snapshot of someone coming by and being surprised by your monkeys!

★ Just a thought: If you ever need to get rid of a bunch of stuffed animals, get a big box. Write something like, "Free puppies, kittens, etc." on the box, and then sit holding the box outside a grocery store. (The fun will come from seeing people's expressions as they look at you!)

A MATTER OF PERSPECTIVE

There is a tower in Italy called the Leaning Tower of Pisa. Because it's a cool tower, and because it's leaning, tourists (like me!) enjoy taking pictures where it looks like someone is standing in front of the tower and "holding" it up. This works because of *perspective*. If the person in a photo stands close enough to the camera lens, whatever is in the background of the picture will appear to be *smaller* than the person . . . even if, in reality, the object in the background is *much bigger* than the person!

Of course, you can create this trick photo with all sorts of things, not just Italian towers! To get the trick to work, it's important to have the person standing in the exact right spot. Be sure not to get *too* close with your camera, or else the photo will look unrealistic. Also, try not to show the palms of the person's hands "touching" the object they are holding up.

You can also do this trick with things besides objects! For example, try creating a shot where it looks like someone is holding a tiny person in his or her hands (the person in the background needs to be in a dip or on a hill).

BED JUMPING!

In case you didn't know, there are entire books and Web sites devoted to pictures of people jumping on beds. Many people do this in hotel rooms! For some reason, this makes it more fun. (Probably because people don't usually get in as much trouble for jumping on the bed in their hotel room.)

Note: If you have no bed to jump on, a trampoline may be substituted. However, this is not as fun, because you're SUPPOSED to jump on a trampoline!

Important Safety Note: Never, ever, ever jump on a bed that's close to a window. EVER.

You can take bed-jumping shots using the timer on your camera, or you can have someone else take the picture. At first, the goofiness of being caught midair with your hair flying all over the place will be enough to keep you laughing. But soon you'll want more challenges!

Clothing: If you have nice clothes, put them on for your shot. Seeing a well-dressed person bouncing in the air is funnier than seeing someone in a T-shirt and shorts. (Also, for some reason, wearing a shower cap in your photo is cool, especially if you strike a "flying superhero" pose with it!)

The Relaxed Pose: "Yeah, I'm just hanging out . . . in the air."

Two-Bed Exchange: If there are two people and two beds, try to get a shot of each person flying over the other person's bed.

The Cloud: Gather all the pillows you can find, and then jump up in the air while holding the pillows with your arms and hands. The point is to try to conceal your body behind the pillows as the photo is taken.

Photo from the Head: If you set up the camera at the head of the bed, the person can run and leap at the bed for an "Incoming!" type of shot.

PHOTOSHOPPED FREAKAZOIDS

I've got almost no computer skills, but even I can cut, resize, and paste stuff. And if you can do that too, try experimenting with some of these really weird photo tricks.

The Baby Head Switcheroo: While switching your mom's head with your dad's might be funny, there is NOTHING weirder than switching an adult's head with

a baby's! After you cut and paste the heads, be sure to make the baby's head larger and the adult's head smaller. Spooky!

Upside-Down Face: Few things are as bizarre as clipping someone's face, turning it around, and then pasting it back into their head. To top off this coolness, rotate the picture so that the face is looking at

you normally, but the chin is at the top of the picture and the hair is at the bottom!

Upside-Down Features: This is a little tougher than clipping out an entire face. To do this, take a picture of someone smiling. Now take that photo and flip around the two eyes (individually) and the mouth. They should be in the same place, but upside down. Now take the photo and turn it so that the chin is at the top of the picture and the hair is at the bottom. It actually might look pretty normal—until you turn it around so that the head is right-side up. (Then it's just FREAKY!)

TACKY PORTRAITS

I just realized that I've had a bulletin board in my room my entire life. Bulletin boards are cool because I can use them to tack up photos, postcards, and stickers. But I've never actually tacked a *bulletin* on one!

Weird.

Anyway, have someone take a picture of you where you're screaming in pain. (Fake pain, not real pain. What kind of book do you think this is?) Pretend you're having a spear driven through part of your body. Hold your hands over that part of your body and have someone take your picture.

Now print up the photo. When you tack it to your bulletin board, you're going to push the tack through the part of your body that you were holding in the photo. That way, it looks like the tack is actually causing you the discomfort!

HOLIDAY CARD

Some people mail cards to their family members and friends in December. If your family does this, try to convince your parents to use the following picture as the family portrait.

First, you have to pick the people who will cry in the picture. Don't worry, they're going to be faking it! If there are two kids in your family, the oldest one will cry. If there are four kids, the three oldest ones will all be crying. If you're an only child, your dad or mom will cry.

Now, the idea for the picture is that you have hogged all of the [insert cool items here]. For example, let's say that you have an older brother. And let's also say that you have a pizza at your house. Wait until you get down to the last two pieces, and you're ready for the photo. Grab one slice of pizza and get ready to eat it. But also grab the OTHER slice so that it's clearly in your possession.

Now give the camera a smug little smile as you take a bite of pizza. While you do this, your older brother should be standing next to you, crying!

This idea can work with all sorts of things, not just pizza. For example, let's say you have two kittens at home. Take a picture where you're petting both of the kittens and looking smugly at the camera while your older brother cries. (You get the idea.)

Realistic Crying Tips: If you're going to be the designated "crier," do this before you take the photo: rub your face briskly with your hands so that your face is red.

Be sure to squinch your eyes shut. And it helps if you're actually making a crying sound (as in *"Waaah!"*) when the picture is taken. Trust me.

TREE PATCH

*T*he next time you're walking around your neighborhood, look at the trees. (Crazy, I know!) See if you can find a tree that has a large bit of bark missing on its trunk. This can happen when branches are cut off, or just because of weird growth patterns.

Did you find one? If so, get some wrapping paper or patterned cloth. (The brighter and more colorful, the better.) You'll also need some scissors, a pen, and maybe a staple gun. (A really good stapler could also work.)

Take your supplies and approach the bare patch on the tree trunk. Don't be afraid—it's just a tree!

Stretch the paper or cloth over the bare patch. Use your pen to trace the outline of the patch onto the paper or cloth. Then use the scissors to cut out the paper or cloth. Now hold it up to the bare patch. Fit the paper or cloth into place, and then staple it to the tree trunk!

Now step back. It should look like the bark has been stripped back to reveal the tree's colorful center!

THE "I'M NOT HEADLESS, I'M NECKLESS!" SHOT

For both of these pictures, you'll need two people and someone with a camera (like you!).

Buried in Sand!

For this photo, you need to be at the beach or some other mega-sandy spot where you can bury someone up to his or her neck without too much work. (And if you ARE at the beach, make sure to do this in a spot away from the incoming tide!)

After getting your volunteer properly covered in sand, stand on his "face" side with your camera. Now have the second person stand with his back to you and his feet on either side of the first person's head. Have the second person take a half step back with each foot and bend over. Reaching down, the second person should pretend to be grabbing the ears of the buried first person's head.

As long as the bending person's head isn't visible, take the picture. The resulting photo will look as if someone lost his head and is bending down to pick it up!

To get the same effect another way, have your first person squat or kneel behind a bed or some other large piece of furniture. This person should have only his head (facing you) exposed. Your second person sits with his back to you NEXT to the person's head. With one arm, he reaches over to grab "his" head with his hand.

Headless Bookends!

The setup for this picture requires you to set up a board or a shelf between two chairs (or sawhorses, or whatever). Two people will sit or stand so that their chins can comfortably rest on the shelf. These two people can stand anywhere from a foot to five feet apart, but closer is probably better.

Get some books and prop them up between the two heads! Once you have your "bookends" properly placed, step back. As you take the picture, try to frame it so that the bottom frame of the picture is the edge of the shelf. (That way, you won't see the bodies of your bookends below.) But even if you can't frame it perfectly, it's no big deal—you can always crop the picture later!

STREEETCH SHOT!

Have a person lie down with his head at one end of a sofa. Have another person lie down so that his feet are at the other end of the sofa. Now cover the first person with a big blanket from the shoulders down. The blanket should leave only the feet of the other person uncovered. Snap away!

THE GRAND FINALE!

This is a great picture, but it takes a certain amount of setup. For starters, you need two big people and one little person.

Got them? Next, it would be nice if all three people were wearing those uniforms that martial arts students wear— they're generally called *keikogi*, or just *gi* for short. Anyway, your models don't need to have on an official *gi*, but it would be nice. And if just the two big people have *gis* (or just the little person does!), that also works.

Now, think of the posture that karate instructors get into when they punch a board in half. In demonstrations, one person holds a board with both hands. Then the other person stands in front of the board and punches, kicks, or head butts the board, breaking it in half.

What you're going to do is take a picture of that moment, but instead of feet or fists, you're going to use a person's head to break the board. So think about what that broken board looks like! Yep, it's wood, and it's broken in half.

What you need to do is find a short board like that and saw it in half! Use a vise or sawhorse, and ask for help if you need it. When you're done, you're ready for these steps:

1. A big person is going to pick up the little person.

2. The second big person is going to pick up the two pieces of the broken board and hold them together as if they weren't broken at all.

3. The first big person is going to hold the little person like a battering ram, with the little person's head pointing forward into the board.

4. The second big person will hold the boards at chest height while bracing himself for impact by spreading his legs and making a face.

5. The first big person will step forward and gently push the little person's head against the broken board.

6. As the little person's head pushes against the wood, the board will begin to "break." This is when you take the picture! If possible, the big people should look as if the impact is tremendous. The little person can either grimace in pain or wave at the camera—whichever is funnier!

DEEP THOUGHTS

You know what's really fun? Thinking about the world around you! There are so many odd and interesting things in it, if we only take the time to notice them. In fact, I've heard that comedians often get good material just by standing on a street corner and watching people pass by.

Imagine you're people-watching in New York. It's winter, and snow starts falling to the ground. Wow! People come out of storefronts to look at the lights and the beautiful snow. Yep, there sure are a lot of people!

You're already having fun, but maybe you could have more! So you roll up a snowball and throw it at your friend, sister, or father. If you're lucky, that person will throw a snowball back at you. And if you can get enough people involved, pretty soon there will be a huge snowball fight going on!

How fun would it be to have a snowball fight in Times Square? REALLY fun. Good thinking!

Another fun thing to think about are life's deep questions. Ever since you could talk, you've probably asked questions about the world around you using "who, what, when, where" and especially "why." Your questions were so good that adults had trouble answering them! You know, like:

★ Who invented time?

★ What is the difference between moss and lichen?

★ When did the sea get salty?

★ Where did that baby come from?

★ Why is the sky blue?

And now that you're older, you ask even tougher questions, such as: Can a bar of soap get dirty? Luckily, there are experts available to answer these difficult questions. But even experts like the mysterious person known only as "the Explainer" sometimes get asked questions he is unable or unwilling to answer. Like these!

★ Why do panda bear names (Ling Ling, Tuan Tuan, Yuan Yuan) always get doubled?

★ Is it possible to collect all the cookie dough in Chocolate Chip Cookie Dough ice cream and actually bake cookies from it?

★ Why do all national anthems sound like European marching-band music?

★ If the elastic band on my underwear loses its spring, but the underwear is barely used, what should I do with it?

★ Let's say that an astronaut on the way to Mars had a baby. If the father were of a different nationality than the mother, what would the citizenship of the baby be?

★ Would it be better if things were better, and worse if things were worse, or better if things were worse and worse if things were better?

★ How would the law punish Siamese twins if one of the twins committed murder without the other being involved? (Actually, "the Explainer" did sort of answer this one: "No one knows.")

BRAIN FUN!

Go into a library or bookstore and ask, "Do you have any books about bookshelves?" This may blow the clerk's mind. Or the clerk might be so impressed that he gives you a free copy of this book. (On the other hand, he might just say, "ALL of our books are on bookshelves"!)

IMAGINARY DILEMMAS

S tretching your mind is incredibly fun. A great way to do this is to practice "imaginary dilemmas." This is where you imagine a problem that forces you to make a difficult choice. The dilemma makes you think really hard about the best way to react! While these are fun to think about by yourself, it's also interesting to discuss dilemmas with others.[1]

For starters, here's one. Let's say you could make a phone call to yourself at anytime in the past. The phone call will

1. But avoid spoilsports who say, "If it's imaginary, then it hasn't happened. Why should I care?" You want people who will play along!

only last one minute. And to save time, let's say that you don't have to spend the whole minute trying to convince yourself that it's not a crank call!

So, what would you say to yourself? I started thinking about this, and I came up with a list of all the different things I wanted to WARN my past self about.

1. Don't eat more than one Flintstones vitamin a day.

2. If you wipe out on your face while waterskiing, the water will go up your nose and into your brain.

3. Unless you want a nice scar, don't pet strange cats.

But then I asked a friend of mine what she would do in this dilemma. She thought for a moment and said, "I would just tell myself to have a happy life."

You can imagine my surprise! "What? No warnings? Aren't you even going to tell her where you live, or what your job is?"

She shook her head. "Just like anyone else, I need to learn from my mistakes. And if I tell myself what happens in the future, it will take the fun out of getting there."

Wow. I never thought about it that way!

THINKING ABOUT WORDS!

Using words like "no", "not," or "nothing" twice in a sentence (Example: "I don't have no money") gives it the *opposite* meaning. ("So you DO have money!"). But what did basketball player Rasheed Wallace mean with this *triple*-negative: *"I ain't changing nothing for nobody"*?

Positive words like "yes" or "for sure" can be used as much as you want without changing the meaning of what you're saying. Yet through the magic of sarcasm, the phrase "Yeah, right" somehow takes two positive words and then gives them a negative meaning!

Okay, here's a different dilemma. It's probably illegal where you live to drive a car or ride a bike while talking on a cell phone. So let's say you're out riding your skateboard when you see a mean kid on a tricycle rob a bank. As the robber makes his getaway ("Look how fast he's pedaling!"), you have some choices to make. You can:

a. Follow the kid on your skateboard. (But it could be dangerous!)

b. Call the police on your cell phone. (But by the time they arrive, that kid will be long gone!)

c. Follow the kid on your skateboard while calling the police and giving them directions where the little criminal is headed. (But that's probably illegal. Plus, while you're distracted on your cell phone, you could get run over by a kid on a scooter!)

So what do you do? Remember, there is no wrong answer— except for one that is really dumb! While you're chewing on that, here's another good dilemma: Imagine you were given $100. Sweet! But you have to give your best friend (or sister or brother) part of the money.

You get to decide on how much ($70?) or how little ($3?) to give the person. But the catch is that the other person has to AGREE to take the money! If he or she doesn't agree, then neither one of you gets any money at all.

You would think that the other person would take ANY amount because it's free money! And you'd be wrong. Studies show that in lots of cases, the other person will try to get more money than you're offering. And if you won't give in, then that person won't take the money, and you both get zilch.

Why? The person may be someone who values fairness. ("Let's split it 50-50!") Or he may think of himself as a good negotiator. ("I won't settle for less than $35. Take it or leave it.") Or he may be trying to get payback for what he sees as an insult. ("You're offering me a crummy $40? Forget it! How do you like them apples?")

Now, try to predict what kind of deal some of your friends and family members would insist on. Write down their names and amounts and then explain the hypothetical situation to them. And if you don't think a hypothetical situation will work, try a junior version of the game with a very real $10.[2]

Not only is it fun to consider imaginary dilemmas, but it can also be useful. For example, let's imagine that you are on a crowded escalator. Suddenly, it breaks down. How will you ever be able to save all the stranded people?

IMAGINARY FUN!

Imagine what a group of puppies or kittens would say to each other. Would it be like this?

"You're so cute!"

"Stop! You're the cutest one here."

"Nope, I just got a cavity from how sweet you are!"

"Why, you little cutie."

"Who's the cute puppy? YOU'RE the cute puppy!"

"I may be cute, but you're the CUTEST."

"Let's roll around on the floor now."

"Totally!"

2. To get the cash, just write to me care of my publisher. (Better yet, just write my publisher!)

Below are even more dilemmas. Think of them like riddles that have more than one answer. And the answer you give is only as good as the reasons you have to *explain* your answer. (That's where the thinking comes in!)

★ You hate cheaters! But during class, you see your brother cheating on a test. Dang it! And he's not even being sly! So would you turn him in? It *is* probably the right thing to do . . . but what about the fact that he's your BROTHER? (Extra credit: What if you decided not to turn in your brother, and then you saw a known tattletale watching your brother cheating. Would you try to talk the tattletale out of turning him in?)

★ Hiking in the woods, you come upon a pit of quicksand. Yes! But hey, there are two people stuck in it! One of them is your favorite teacher from school, while the other is that kid you don't like very much. Both are yelling, "Help me!" and they're both close to going under. Looking around, you find a stick long enough to reach one of them. What do you do?

★ You're in a spelling bee. *Yes!* And you're in the finals. It's just you and some kid you don't even know. The other kid misses a word. That means if you get your word right, you win!

You're asked to spell the word "meep." But as you spell the word, you realize you made a mistake. ("Meep. M-e-p-e. Meep.") But the judges give you credit for the correct spelling. You won! Or did you? Would you take the trophy? Or would you tell the judges there'd been a mistake?

SCHOOL FUN!

The next time you have a question in class, try this:

You: I have a question.

Teacher: What is it?

You: An interrogative statement used to test knowledge. But that's not important right now.

Then ask your question!

★ You're wearing a new dress shirt and pants that will disintegrate if they get wet.[3] *Yes!* But suddenly, your archenemy jumps out from behind a bush and throws a water balloon at you. Just as that happens, a man pushing a baby carriage steps into the path of the flying water balloon. Nooo! If you do nothing, the poor baby will get wet. But if you step in front of the water balloon, YOU'LL get wet. Your clothes will disintegrate, and you'll be standing there naked! What's the right thing to do?

3. I did mention this is imaginary, right?

THINKING ABOUT ADS

One interesting thing to pay attention to is advertising. Let's say you're in a toy store and you start looking through its catalog of new toys. Sure, you could just be distracted by the bright colors and cool-sounding names ("I've GOT to get a Gorilla-Bot!"), but what if you actually paid attention to the ways the toys are ADVERTISED?

That's what some Swedish sixth graders did. They discovered that when advertisements showed boys playing with toys, the boys were being active (running, jumping, exploding). "We're superheroes!"

But when advertisements showed girls playing with toys, the girls were shown as being passive—sitting, standing, or even lying down. "We're princesses! And princesses don't run." Plus, the boys were shown playing with only certain kinds of toys (the macho ones), while the girls got anything girly.

So the Swedish kids filed a complaint with a Swedish watchdog group.[4] And the watchdog group agreed! It found that the advertisements discriminated based on gender and counteracted "positive social behavior, lifestyles, and attitudes." Everybody hoped this would encourage advertisers to be more thoughtful.

4. The watchdog group is called the *Reklamombudsmannen*. Whew!

Pretty cool, huh? Those kids made a difference just by thinking about the world around them! But now I have a complaint: I think that toy stores are ageist. Yeah, they discriminate against older people! When was the last time you saw an ad showing a grown man playing with toy trucks?

★ LeBron James is a really good basketball player. Sure, he practices hard, but the facts are that he's tall, he can jump really high, and he has lightning-fast reflexes. These are like superpowers that he was born with! Since LeBron didn't "earn" these abilities, the millions of dollars he makes should be donated to charity. (He should be left with just enough to live on.)

If you disagree with the above statement, that means you think LeBron "owns" his natural abilities. Okay, fine! If we own our own bodies, then what if I want to sell my kidney? I don't want to donate it—that would mean I'd get nothing for my kidney, and I'm kind of using it right now.

I want to sell my kidney for, say, $15,000. But there's a problem. In most countries, it's illegal to sell your own internal organs. What a rip-off! If LeBron can "sell" his basketball ability, can you explain why I shouldn't be able to sell something I own?

★ Many people really need organ transplants. But there is always a shortage of organs from donors. Should the organs that are available go to the highest bidder? If not, how should they be assigned?

★ If your best friend had a really bad cough and needed a very expensive medication to get better, would you shoplift the medicine?

★ Shipwreck! Luckily, the captain is your mom. Unluckily, she can either save you and leave the other passengers behind, or she can save them and leave you to try to survive on the boat. What do you say to her?

★ Suppose you have to move to either Boston or Las Vegas. If you move to Boston, you'll fall in love and get married. If

PORTRAIT IN DEEP THINKING!

There was once a man named Emmanuel Kant (1724–1824) who got into trouble for writing about religion. Religion and politics have always been very touchy subjects. In Kant's case, he had to go before the king and defend himself.

Ulp. One false move, and it could have been curtains for Kant!

Kant chose his words carefully. Knowing the king was a very old man, Kant basically said, "As your majesty's faithful subject, I will stop writing about annoying topics." This worked!

The king passed away a few years later. And then Kant could write whatever he wanted, since he was no longer the king's "faithful subject"!

you move to Vegas, you'll get rich but stay single. Should you move to Vegas, if being rich gives you more pleasure than being married?

★ Little Timmy is a troublemaker. Luckily, his best friend Hurley is always around to stop him from getting into trouble. As a result, even though Little Timmy wants to create mischief, he actually does a lot of good things instead. Does that make Little Timmy a good person?

Wait, there's more! Suppose Hurley moved away. With Hurley's good influence gone, Little Timmy plants a stink bomb with a timer somewhere near the kindergarten class. That stink bomb will go off in an hour unless the principal can find it first. Those poor little kids! What should the principal be allowed to do to get the information out of Little Timmy?

a. Put gum in his hair.
b. Get mad at him.
c. Play elevator music REALLY loud.
d. Nothing.

★ How should a person get to own something? Does he or she have to work for it? What if a disabled person needs a wheelchair but can't buy or build one herself? Does she have a right to the wheelchair anyway? If so, why? If not, what do you think is going to happen to her?

THE WRONG DEFINITION OF FUN

Hey, I have a question: Have you ever seen two people get in an argument about a topic they disagree on? Why do they do that? Have you EVER seen someone change his mind in one of these arguments?

If people who argue were *honestly* seeking the truth, this is what would happen: Each person would speak. The other person would listen carefully. And then the two people would come to a reasonable agreement. But that almost never happens! I think this is because most people don't think it's fun to change their mind. Instead, they argue and show off how stubborn they are!

But from now on, let's all pretend that it's fun to actually listen to the other person and understand their point of view. That way, the argument won't get personal. (Plus, if you listen well, at the very least, you'll have a better argument to use against the other person!)

If you end up changing your mind about the topic at hand, that means you've probably learned something! And here's the greatest secret of all time: LEARNING THINGS IS THE MOST FUN YOU CAN EVER HAVE! (Besides throwing water balloons at your friends.)

BONUS. DEEP QUESTION!

Have you ever looked at an orange and wondered, "Is this fruit called an orange because it's orange, or is the color orange orange because of this orange?"

The quick answer is that orange is orange because it is orange, and orange is orange because of the orange.

Oops! My bad. Here's a quicker way to say it: The fruit came first. The word for the color came from the fruit.

Next time: the tangerine!

LAUGHTER RULES

How many times in your life has someone tried to get you to laugh? I'm going to take a guess and say 596 times. And that means you know firsthand how hard it can be NOT to laugh. Sure, you can concentrate on something super-sad and serious. (Try imagining that you lost this book, for instance.)

But even when you think you have it beat, laughter can strike like a bolt of lightning! And this is not always fun . . . or comfortable. Like me, you may know someone who has laughed so hard, he spit up juice, shot milk out of his nose, or peed his pants.[1] (There should be a special word for that last one. "Paughed"? "Leed"?)

---

1. And if you don't know someone like that, you may BE someone like that!

"Cracking up" like this is a particular danger for actors. In fact, actors have even come up with a special word for someone who starts laughing in the middle of a scene: *corpsing*. This word got started by actors who were supposed to be playing dead bodies, aka "corpses." But for some totally illogical reason, actors who were *supposed* to be holding still and looking dead would sometimes giggle and then get hysterical with laughter.

You can see how that might ruin a scene.

While it stinks trying to perform onstage while your fellow actor is corpsing, it's fun for the rest of us! People tend to laugh along with someone else, even if they have no idea what that person is laughing about. For example, I love it when DVDs have outtakes of actors corpsing. These make me laugh harder than the movie's actual jokes!

Performers say there is no way to predict what will make someone start to corpse. But there is a downside to this dreadful condition. You see, while everyone will laugh along on the first, second, third, and even *fourth* times an actor corpses, after that, they just get annoyed.

But strangely, having everyone else get annoyed does not usually help the corpsing actor STOP laughing. In fact, it can make the problem worse! If you've ever gotten hysterical when everyone else was looking at you with a mixture of disgust and wonder, you know this is true!

Of course, you don't have to be an actor to corpse. Years ago, I was watching a British comedy show called *The Goodies*. During a skit, a Scottish man in a kilt used his bagpipes to defend himself from a giant pudding. (This was *really* funny, trust me.) I giggled, and as the Scotsman's bagpipe kung fu grew kookier, I started laughing. Hard. When someone came into the room and asked me what was so funny, all I could do was helplessly point at the TV with tears streaming down my face.

I was not the only person who corpsed when I saw that skit. A man named Alex Mitchell also laughed really hard at it. Then he fell over, stone dead. Was this a tragedy? Maybe! Even so, Alex's wife sent a very nice letter to the staff at *The Goodies*, thanking them for giving her hubbie such a pleasant send-off. (Makes sense! If you have to die, why not die laughing?)

Of course, laughter is not usually fatal, but some people do have a medical problem with laughing. You see, there is a condition called *cataplexy*. A person who has cataplexy will suddenly collapse if she starts laughing very hard. That's right, a cataplectic might chortle and then have a sudden physical collapse. She is rendered helpless by laughter! (In this situation, laughter is *not* the best medicine. In fact, it would be important to find the best medicine to treat the laughter!)

Anyway, cataplectics naturally try to avoid funny situations. One sufferer named Kay Underwood says that sometimes her friends "good-naturedly" try to make her laugh. They like to see her fall over, I guess. To protest this bad behavior, the next time one of my friends tries to make me laugh, I'm not going to—just to spite 'em!

Either that or I'll fall off my chair, shooting milk out of my nose.

HAIL TO THE CHIEF!

Get your hands on a long, narrow red rug. Then roll it up and keep it by the front door. When you see someone approaching your house, run out and unroll the "red carpet." Then grandly invite the visitor to enter. (If your visitor asks what *else* is part of the red carpet treatment, tell him not to push it.)

Researchers have carefully studied what happens inside our brain when we laugh. They've found that when something funny happens, your brain has to go through all its memories to compare what you *just* saw to everything else you have *ever* seen. Then the brain tries to solve the problem of whether what it saw was funny. Then the emotions have to kick in and help create laughter.

So, from a general viewpoint, what kinds of things make us laugh? Well, you'd be surprised! For one humor study, scientists watched people in shopping centers and carefully took notes. They found that fewer than one laugh out of five was because of a joke or funny story. Most of the laughter happened when people said "hello" or "good-bye" to each other.

So we laugh when greeting or leaving one another? Weird!

Here are some other things that can get people laughing:

★ Things that happen during times of danger and excitement.

Captain Benjamin Tupper of the US Army National Guard has an interesting take on this. He found himself fighting in some very dangerous battles in Afghanistan. Although there's nothing funny about getting shot at, Tupper wrote that "some of the funniest things happen when your life is on the line and you do something stupid. [And] when you retell the stories, you'll never laugh harder."

★ Things we find to be true.

When you laugh at something, you often don't have time to think first. Your laughter is almost automatic! So if someone likes the Portland Trail Blazers, they will tend to laugh at jokes about their rivals, the Los Angeles Lakers. It's only natural!

★ Jokes where you "had to be there."

Personally, I don't understand what's up with all this "you had to be there" humor. Are all these people telling geography jokes? Ha! Get it? It's a "you had to be there" joke! So if you don't get it, you had to be there. (Heh heh, *ouch.*)

★ Things that contain an element of surprise.

But despite the general rules, not everyone finds the same things funny. You see, there are two kinds of people in the world: male and female.

Humor research shows that little kids, boys, and men like very simple types of humor. Often called "slapstick" humor, this is the kind of laughter that comes from people falling down, telling poop jokes, or making weird faces.

Girls, and especially women, prefer humor that comes from memories, personal information, relationships, and stories. In short, women like complicated humor. Why? Because they're smart!

Remember to watch other people carefully when they laugh. Researchers have found that if a person is *really* laughing, he will close his eyes for a moment. If a person laughs *without* closing his eyes, he's *faking* it! He's either doing this to be polite, or it's a "no soap, radio" thing (see p. 157).

KNOW YOUR LAUGHERS!

People often laugh using words like "Ha!" or "Hee hee!" Long ago, followers of *geloscopy* believed the word you used to laugh revealed part of your personality! People who said "Ha!" when they laughed were considered to be honest but undependable, while people who said "Hee!" were considered to be sad or simpleminded. People who said "Ho!" were thought of as brave and generous, while people who said "Huu!" were supposed to be untrustworthy. Ho, ho, ho! Here are some other laughing styles:

THE WORST SENSE OF HUMOR IN THE WORLD?

The people of Germany have never been known for their sense of humor. They are a serious people! For example, here is a joke that Germans like to tell. Amazingly, the joke is about how Germans don't have a sense of humor!

"Knock, knock."

"Who's there?"

"The police. I'm afraid there's been an accident. Your husband is in the hospital."

See? Not funny! And get this: I just read a news article about a German woman who called the police with an emergency. She had just returned from a walk when she thought she could hear someone being tortured. The police investigated immediately! They quickly discovered the man who was being tortured. His name was Roland Hofmann. He had taken a humorous book with him on a walk, and had stopped to read it. The horrible "tortured" sounds the woman caller had heard was Roland's laughter!

A police spokesperson said, "We realize that people think the sound of Germans laughing is unusual, but we're sure the caller meant well." Hey, this could give us a new German knock-knock joke!

"Knock, knock."

"Who's there?"

"The police. Please stop laughing. Your neighbors find your sounds of joy incredibly disturbing."

The Oxygen Tank: When amused, this person wheezes like she can't get a good breath of air.

The Script Reader: This person really does laugh, but they're using words to do it. (For example, my dad actually goes "Hee, hee, hee." The Script Reader is a little bit like . . .

The Barker: "Ha! Haha! Ha!"

The Silent Chuckler: It's a little weird to make this person laugh because it takes a while to know if they ARE laughing. There may be a moment of quiet, followed by the person saying, "Now THAT was funny."

The Donkey: No offense, but if someone brays with a "hee-haw" sound, this is the label they end up with!

The Infectious Laugher: Merry peals of laughter ring throughout the room, and even if you're in a bad mood, you find yourself smiling. Scientists have not found an antidote for this laughing infection. But why would they want one?

The Sarcastic Laugher: Not good! If we work together, we can stomp out "Ha. Ha. Ha" or "Har-de-har-har" or "That was so funny, I forgot to laugh."

The Startlingly Loud Laugher: This person's chortles are so loud, he can make babies cry, dogs drop their bones, and shoppers run for the exit.

The Special Effects Laugher: I have heard people warble, whinny, whistle, and wheeze when laughing. (And sometimes they even snort!)

The Sobber: Wow. Is this person laughing or crying?

JOKES

I've divided the jokes in this chapter into a few different categories. The first category contains some of the most simpleminded jokes of all time. Then we progress to jokes that are just plain old simpleminded. Enjoy!

JOKES SO DUMB, NO COWARD CAN TELL THEM

Believe it or not, I admire people who tell dumb jokes. By doing so, they show that they are not self-conscious. That means they don't care what other people think of them. In short, people who tell dumb jokes are the bravest of all. They are our heroes, and to honor their courage, here are their jokes.

Oh, I almost forgot: Many dumb jokes have a question-and-answer format. This is helpful for comic timing. Here's an example of what I'm talking about:

You: Ask me if I'm a tree.
Friend: Why would I ask if you're a tree?
You: No, seriously, just play along. Ask me if I'm a tree.
Friend (*sighing*): FINE. Are you a tree?
You: No.

Man, I *love* that sort of thing! The thing that makes it funny is how it plays with what a person *thinks* is going to happen. Here's another one:

A boy sees a girl cupping something with her hands.
Boy: What do you have there?
Girl: Guess!

Boy: Is it a rock?

Girl: No.

Boy: A flower? Nothing? Money?

Girl: No, no, and no.

Boy *(tired of the game)*: Is it a horse?

Girl *(opening her hands and peeking inside)*: What color?

You get the idea! And now, let me share more material that will take bravery for you to share with others:

Q: What's yellow, smooth, and dangerous?
A: Shark-infested custard.

Q: Where does our president keep his armies?
A: Up his sleevies.

Q: Why did the chicken cross the road?
A: To help fight the fire.

Q: Why did the lion cross the road?
A: To get a free roast chicken.

Q: What's yellow, smells like bananas, and sits at the bottom of a tree?
A: Monkey barf.

Q: What kind of primate can fly?
A: A hot-air baboon.

Man in grocery store: Your frozen chickens are all too small. Do they get any bigger?
Clerk: No, sir, they're dead.

Q: Why did Captain Kirk pee on the ceiling?
A: So he could go where no man had gone before.

Q: What's invisible and smells like carrots?
A: Bunny farts.

Police officer: Why did you park in this No Parking zone?
Driver: The sign said FINE FOR PARKING!

Q: What's the difference between roast beef and pea soup?
A: *Anyone* can roast beef!

Q: What is boring, annoying, and you have to live with it all your life?
A: Your brother!

Q: If H2O is on the inside of a fire hydrant, then what's on the outside?

A: K9P.

Q: When is the sentence "Objects In Mirror Are Closer Than They Appear" the last thing you want to read?

A: When the mirror's on your tricycle and the "object" is an angry pit bull.

KNOCK-KNOCK JOKES

Knock-knock jokes have the same kind of built-in rhythm as question–and–answer jokes, and that's why kids love them. (Except when they hate them!)

"Knock, knock."

"Who's there?"

"Yeah."

"Yeah, who?"

"Hey, you're glad to see me!"

"Knock, knock."

"Who's there?"

"The Interrupting Cow."

"The Interru—"

"Moooooo!"

"Knock, knock."

"Who's there?"

"The Interrupting Starfish."

"The Interrupting Starfish wh—"

Spread your fingers and place your hand over the person's face.

Hot Tip: If a kid keeps working you with knock-knock jokes and you're tired of playing, do this.

Kid: Knock, knock!

You: Use the doorbell.

Kid: Uh . . . ding-dong.

You: Nobody's home.

Or better yet:

Kid: Knock, knock!

You: Come in.

COOLER JOKES

A more advanced joke often has a little story to it, or maybe a tricky punch line that makes a person think. And sometimes a joke like this may have actually happened! Take, for example, this conversation I once overheard in a classroom.[2]

2. I overheard it because I was the teacher.

Student: I need to go to P.E. now.

Teacher (*hearing the word "pee"*): Really? Can you hold it?

Student (*puzzled*): No, I am supposed to be there now.

Teacher: I don't understand. You mean you are *scheduled* for it?

Student: Well, yeah, I'm always supposed to go to P.E. at this time.

Teacher (*whispering*): Do you have a, uh, condition I should know about?

Student: What? No! Why?

Teacher: I was just wondering why you have an appointment to pee at the same time every day.

Student: *P.E.! P.E.!* Not pee.

Teacher: Oh, P.E.! Ha ha. Ouch. Yes, you can go.

• •

A guy walks into the library and loudly says, "I'd like a BURGER, FRIES, and a COKE."

"Shhh!" the librarian whispers. "This is a LIBRARY."

"Oh, I'm sorry," the guy quietly answers. "I'd like a burger, fries, and a coke."

• •

A boy who had to share a bedroom with his brother Timmy was talking to his mom.

"Timmy has been driving me crazy. He's been pretending he's a refrigerator!"

His mom laughed. "How does that bother you?"

"Timmy sleeps with his mouth open," the boy replied. "And the little light is keeping me awake!"

• •

A teacher told his class that he ran a marathon over the weekend. A girl raised her hand. "My mom's in great shape," she said. "She started running last year, and she hasn't stopped since.

"Wow! Hey, I've never met your mom," the teacher replied.

"No surprise," said the girl. "We don't know where she is."

• •

A father caught his baby daughter just as she swallowed a big magnet. The dad freaked out and drove her to the emergency room. After X-rays, a doctor spoke with him.

"Don't worry," the doctor said. "Your daughter should pass the magnet tomorrow."

The man made a face. *Dang it!* He didn't want to search his daughter's poop looking for the magnet. "How will I know when that's happened?" he asked.

The doctor thought for a moment. "Try sticking her to the refrigerator," she said. "When your daughter falls off, you'll know."

• •

A girl is eating a hamburger when she notices a dog is watching every move she makes. The girl breaks off a piece of the hamburger and calls the dog over. It politely advances.

"Speak!" the girl commands. "Speak!"

"Under the circumstances," the dog replies, "I hardly know what to say."

• •

A teacher was trying to explain to some third graders how to multiply numbers, but he could tell they weren't getting it.

"Okay, who knows what three times three is?" he asked.

One of his best students raised his hand and said, "399!"

"Not quite," replied the teacher. "Anyone else?"

"I know!" cried out another student. "It's a trick question. The answer is 'Tuesday!'"

The teacher was rubbing his face in disbelief when he saw his shyest student raise her hand. "Is the answer 'nine?'" she asked shyly.

"Yes!" said the teacher. "Now tell us how you did that."

"It was simple," the girl said. "I just subtracted 399 from Tuesday!"

• •

Three boys were running down the street because they had thrown water balloons at some girls riding their tricycles. The boys ran into an old country store to hide. Each of them hid in an empty sack labeled POTATOES.

When the girls came in, they saw the sacks. One girl kicked a sack with a boy in it. The boy said, "Woof!" hoping the girls would believe he was a dog. Another girl kicked a different sack. The boy inside said, "Meow!" Another girl kicked the third sack.

The boy inside hesitated, and then he called out, "Potatoes!"

• •

A little girl walks into a pet shop and asks, "Do you keep widdle wabbits here?"

The lady who owns the store smiles and says, "Sure, right over here. Do you want a fuzzy widdle brown rabbit or a cute widdle white rabbit?"

The girl shrugs and says, "Either one. My pyfon's not picky."

• •

A woman looking for a parrot went into a pet shop. She saw a beautiful red-and-green parrot, and when she approached it, the bird said, "Hello!" and then began reciting poetry that was so beautiful, the woman cried.

She bought the parrot and took it home. But as soon as the parrot got inside, it began cursing like a sailor! It was "$%^&!" this and "&@&*!" that. The woman was stunned, and then she heard a knock at the door. It was her neighbor! Not wanting to offend anyone, the woman gently put the bird into the refrigerator. "It will just be for a minute," she explained.

After getting rid of her neighbor, the woman returned and let the parrot out of the refrigerator.

"My apologies!" said the parrot. "I'll never speak like that again!" And then the bird added, "And by the way, what did the chicken do?"

• •

A woman sits down on a park bench to enjoy the sunny weather. Seated next to her is an older lady. The two women begin having a pleasant conversation.

After a few moments, the older woman leans in and says, "Can you believe how ugly that fellow over there is?

"Oh," says the younger woman. "That is *my husband*."

"I beg your pardon!" says the older woman. "I do not mean him, I mean that shocking monster behind him."

"And that," replies the younger woman, "is my son."

• •

A girl said to a boy on the bus, "I heard a great joke the other day, but it was about you. I don't want to offend you, so I'll tell it about Little Timmy instead."

The girl told the joke, and when she finished, the boy laughed so hard that tears streamed down his face.

"Wow," the boy gasped. "Little Timmy sure is an idiot!"

• •

The manager of a coffee bar was waiting on customers when a small, angry-looking man came to the front of the line.

"What can I get for you, sir?" the manager asked.

The small, angry-looking man answered, "I want a coffee and I'm not going to pay because I'm not afraid of anybody!"

Since the man was angry and there were people waiting, the manager gave him a free coffee. The next morning, the small, angry-looking man was back. He again demanded a coffee, repeating that he was not going to pay and that he was not afraid of anybody. And again, the manager gave him a coffee.

But enough was enough. Later that day, the manager hired a bouncer named Danny. He weighed three hundred pounds and had tattoos on all visible parts of his body.

The next morning, Danny stood by the order counter, smiling at the customers as the manager took their orders. As expected, the small, angry-looking man came to the front of the line and said, "I want a coffee, and I'm not going to pay because I'm not afraid of anybody!"

Danny stepped forward and leaned way down so that his massive head was near the small, angry-looking man's face. In a deep voice, Danny said, "I'm not afraid of anybody, either."

The small, angry-looking man nodded, turned to the manager, and said, "Make that *two* coffees!"

GROSS HUMOR

Q: What did the cannibal eat when he was on a diet?
A: Children.

• •

Dad: Hey kids, did you notice? I bought a new toilet brush for your bathroom.
Son: We noticed, but we still prefer the paper.

• •

A man walks into his grandma's house. He spots a dish of peanuts on the table and begins eating them. After a while, he says, "Sorry about that, Grandma, but I've eaten almost all of your peanuts."

"That is quite alright," his grandma replies. "Now that I've lost all of my teeth, I can only suck the chocolate coating off of them."

• •

A four-year-old boy comes out of the bathroom, crying because he dropped his toothbrush in the toilet. After his mom fished it out, she threw it away and gave him a new one.

The boy then handed his mother *her* toothbrush and said, "I guess we better throw this one out too, because it fell in the toilet last week."

• •

There was a man who had a big problem. He farted all the time, but he could never smell or hear his farts. He went to the doctor and explained. The doctor considered the problem, and then he wrote the man a prescription and scheduled him to come back for a follow-up appointment.

A week later, the man came back and complained that he was still farting, but now it smelled like rotten eggs! The doctor was pleased, saying, "We've cleared your sinuses! Now we just need to work on your hearing."

• •

A boy named Bud Dudley and his sister Emma were sitting on a couch when the boy farted.

"WHAT WAS THAT?!" Emma asked.

"Fart football," Bud explained. "Seven to o!"

After a while, Emma farted. "Touchdown! Tie score!"

Bud farted again, but quietly, so at first his sister didn't notice. When she did, she cried, "That was silent, Bud Dudly!"[3]

"That's right. It's another touchdown. I'm ahead, 14 to 7."

The sister gave off a bomber. "Tie score!"

3. BONUS: It's a joke within a joke!

Not wanting to lose, Bud tried really, really, really hard to fart, but he pooped instead. The sound was bad. Bud's expression was worse.

"What was that?!" Emma asked.

"Halftime. Switch sides!"

ANTI-HUMOR ("NO SOAP, RADIO!")

Anti-humor is what happens when someone tells a "fake" joke. Not a *bad* joke, but a joke that isn't a joke at all. The person telling the joke also needs at least one other person who is "in" on it who can play along.

The key is that the joke has *no punch line*. Or rather, there is a punch line, but it's not funny. Something like this:

A goose walks into a yogurt shop and asks if he can have non-fat vanilla yogurt. The clerk says, "I've never served yogurt to a goose before." And the goose says, "No soap, radio!"[4]

At this point, the joke teller and his helper laugh like this is the best joke of all time. Now, what about the confused person? He may laugh along and act like he understands the joke. (Know-it-alls and people who want to fit in might do

---

4. Although the punch line can be anything nonsensical, "No soap, radio!" has been used for decades.

this.) Or he may ask what's so funny. (Curious and sincere people do this.)

I guess the person could also think that "No soap, radio" really ıs funny. If you ever find someone like this, he may not understand what humor is . . . or he might just be insane.

LITTLE AUDREY?!

You have now read a wide variety of jokes. However, I have saved a certain category of humor for now. These are the jokes that are about serious, uncomfortable, and even horrible subjects.

Why would anyone even tell jokes like these? Well, the jokes are so wrong, they can sometimes shock a person into laughing out of surprise. And it's quite a tradition; people have been telling and retelling these jokes for centuries. Really! For example, there was a character named Little Audrey who showed up many years ago in jokes like this:

Little Audrey and her grandfather were watching a steamroller fix the road in front of their house. Her grandfather was known as a cheapskate, which was important because suddenly he spotted a coin in the road.

"That's a quarter!" he cried, rushing out to the street. But as he bent to pick it up, the steamroller came along and squished him flat with a horrible sound.

Little Audrey laughed and laughed. She knew all along the coin had only been a nickel!

That's pretty much the idea behind all the Little Audrey jokes. Something dreadful would happen and then Little Audrey would "laugh and laugh." *Yeesh!* Here are some more modern types of Little Audrey jokes. (Jokes about uncomfortable topics are sometimes described as "black humor.")

• •

A man woke up in the hospital after a terrible tricycle accident. He shouted, "Doctor! Doctor! I can't feel my legs!"

The doctor replied, "I know you can't, because I cut off your arms."

• •

Three hunters were walking along in the forest when they came upon a set of tracks.

The first one said, "Those are deer tracks!"

The second one said, "No, those are bear tracks!"

The third one said, "You're both wrong. They're fox tracks."

The three were still arguing when the train hit them.

• •

A girl was at a sold-out concert, but was disappointed to find that her seats were way up in the rafters. Peering down, she could see that there was an aisle seat close to the stage that had been empty for some time.

Taking a gamble, the girl walked down and asked the closest woman if anyone was sitting there.

"No," answered the woman.

"Wow," said the girl, sitting down. "Who would buy such a great seat and then not come to the show?"

"My husband," said the woman. "We were going to come to the concert together, but he passed away."

"I'm so sorry!" cried the girl. "But wasn't there a close friend or relative who could have used the ticket?"

The woman shook her head. "No, they're all at the funeral."

• •

Oy vey. In honor of Little Audrey's achievements, let's end this section with another one of her adventures.

• •

Little Audrey decided to take skydiving lessons. When she was cleared for her first jump, Little Audrey's relatives came from far and wide to watch her big day!

After Little Audrey jumped out of the plane, she was very amused. "I fooled them all!" Little Audrey giggled. "I'm not even wearing a parachute!"

And she laughed and laughed all the way down.

• •

Well, there's no way we can end this chapter like that. Let's see, what else do I have that could work here? Oh, I know!

TURTLE JOKES!

A snail was mugged by two turtles. When the police arrived, they asked the snail to describe what happened.

"I don't know," the snail said. "It all happened so fast!"

• •

A man from Los Angeles walks into an ice-cream shop with a turtle under his arm.

"Cool!" the guy at the counter says. "Where did you get it?"

"Los Angeles," answers the turtle. "They've got millions of them there!"

• •

A turtle crawled into an ice-cream shop and asked a customer to hoist him onto the counter. The waiter took the turtle's order.

"One hot butterscotch sundae," the turtle said.

The waiter brought the turtle his sundae, and the turtle put a ten-dollar bill on the counter. Thinking the turtle wouldn't be able to figure out the correct change, the waiter gave him only one dollar in return.

"You know," said the waiter, "we don't get many turtles in here."

"Well," the turtle replied, "at nine bucks a sundae, you're not likely to get any more."

• •

A woman was driving her Mercedes-Benz down a country road when it started making a weird sound. She pulled over and popped the car's hood, but everything seemed fine.

"The trouble is your carburetor," said a voice. Looking down, the woman saw a turtle with a red dot on the side of his shell.

"Wow, a talking turtle," the woman said. "And you know about cars!" She was so excited, she jumped back into her car and drove (weird noise and all) to the closest gas station. There, she got out and told the attendant what happened.

"Did this turtle have a red spot on the side of his shell?" the attendant asked.

"Yes, he did!" said the woman.

"Aw, I wouldn't pay much attention to him," said the man. "That turtle, he doesn't know as much about cars as he thinks he does."

• •

A family of turtles made some sandwiches and went on a picnic. Because they were turtles, it took them two hours to get to the park, and when they arrived, they realized they'd forgotten a bottle opener.

"Son, you're the fastest," said the father turtle. "Would you go back and get it?"

"But if I leave, you will eat all the sandwiches!" the boy turtle said.

All the turtles promised they would wait for him to return before eating, so off the boy turtle went. Two hours. Then four. Then six.

Finally, the father turtle said, "Something must have held him up. Let's eat!"

But just as they began unwrapping the sandwiches, the boy turtle crawled out from behind a bush. "Ha! I knew this would happen if I left," he said. "So I didn't!"

• •

A woman is sitting at home reading a book about a serial-killer turtle when there's a knock at the door. She opens the door and is shocked to see a turtle sitting on her doorstep!

Alarmed, she picks up the turtle and throws it across the street onto a neighbor's mossy lawn.

Three hours later, there's a knock at the door again. The woman opens the door and the same turtle is sitting on the doorstep!

The turtle says, "So what was THAT about?"

• •

Okay, time for a break. Let's think about this: What *is* a joke? It can be a lot of things, but there's almost no joke that doesn't have some kind of mismatch going on between two out-of-place things. This is often followed by some kind of unexpected ending (the "punch line").

Example: A girl goes to the dentist. After looking at her teeth, the dentist asks, "Do you eat candy apples?"

"Not right now, thank you," says the girl. "I had lunch before coming here."

Okay, it's not the world's greatest joke, but you see the pattern: mismatch, punch line. This pattern can also work in real life. For instance, let's say you're visiting a relative in the hospital. Looking out the window, you notice that some smart aleck out on the sidewalk is dressed up as the Grim Reaper.

And that meanie is waving to the people inside!

Shocked, you turn to your relative and are surprised to find that he is laughing hysterically. He thinks it's FUNNY? And because it was so unexpected to see your relative laughing at the Grim Reaper, you starting laughing, too!

Then you go outside and give the Grim Reaper some sugarless gum.

When scientists observe people laughing like this, they find that the parts of the brain linked to "paying attention" are activated. In other words, for a lot of humor, you have to focus and think. When a person laughs, the part of the brain that deals with pleasure is activated. This means that a good joke can make us *feel* good.

Thanks, Grim Reaper!

Question: Men and women think about humor differently. One group takes longer than the other to decide if something is funny. And once they do, they enjoy the joke more than the other gender. Which one?[5]

5. Women.

THE LOWEST FORM OF FUN

Have you ever heard of a pun? It's a small joke that involves a play of words. So if you see a little kid stub his toe and then start crying, you might say, "Don't worry, I'll call the *toe* truck." This awesome pun will have the little rascal chuckling and forgetting all about his hurt little piggy.

Or it might make him cry harder!

Some people call the pun the "lowest form of humor." But I think the lowest form of humor might be what I call "I betchas." These are challenges that you make to a person that always start with "I bet you that I can . . ." or "I bet you that I can't . . ."

"I betchas" are almost always pretty cheap. That is, few people will be impressed enough by your cleverness that they will laugh out loud. In fact, they might go kick a wall in order to distract themselves from how horrible your "joke" was. But even so, they might have just a little bit of fun!

★ Say to your friend, "You're pretty smart. Why, you're so smart, I bet you can't answer four questions *wrong!*"

Your friend will now want to show you how wrong he can be. To prove him wrong, just lob him three easy questions, like:

What's your mom's first name? (Any answer is correct except for his mom's first name.)

What color is a black bear? (Any answer is correct except for black.)

How long does it take for Saturn to circle the sun? (Any answer is correct, as long as your friend doesn't guess that the answer is 29.46 Earth years, which is indeed how long it takes Saturn to circle the sun.)

After the third question, look slightly confused and casually say, "Wait, that was the THIRD question, right?" Your friend will probably say, "Yes." At that point, you've won, because you just asked your *fourth* question, and your friend answered it correctly!

Ha! Here are a few more "I betchas":

★ Tell your friend, "I bet you I can stand one inch away from you, and you won't be able to touch me." Then have your friend stand in a doorway, close the door, and stand on the other side.

★ Say to your friend, "I bet you I can find a word in the dictionary that is spelled wrong." Then open up a dictionary and look up the word "wrong."

★ Have your friend stand with his heels against the wall. Then throw a twenty-dollar bill on the ground in front of him and say, "I bet you can't pick this up with your hands without moving away from the wall."

★ Shake your head and say, "I bet you are too cowardly to even *try* rubbing your ear with your elbow."

★ Say, "I bet you can't even take off your shoes by yourself." As your friend takes off his shoes, take off your shoes also.

And this last one is a great one. Say to your friend, "I bet I can make lightning and hold it in my hand." Your friend will scoff, or perhaps run off in terror. Assuming your friend scoffs, here's what you will need:

★ A large closet
★ Long fluorescent (NOT incandescent) light bulbs
★ A balloon

Blow up the balloon, and then bring your items (fluorescent bulb, blown-up balloon, friend) into the closet. Hand the balloon to your friend and tell him to rub it on his hair for about twenty seconds. Then hold the balloon up to the end of the fluorescent bulb. Wowsers! See how it lights up? That's because the static electricity from the balloon jumps over to the light bulb.

And that's how you hold lightning in your hand.

RIDDLES?!

Although riddles are cooler than "I betchas," your friends may still think of them as kind of cheap.

But many great writers have enjoyed riddles! For example, J. R. R. Tolkien wrote this riddle, called "Cannot Be Seen."

It cannot be seen, cannot be felt
Cannot be heard, cannot be smelt.
It lies behind stars and under hills,
And empty holes it fills.
It comes first and follows after,
Ends life, kills laughter.

Can you guess the answer? Check the bottom of the page if you give up.[6]

And now, here are a few more riddles:

Q: What do turtles have that no one else can have?
A: Baby turtles.

6. Darkness.

Q: This belongs to you. Even so, without borrowing, stealing, or buying it, your friends use it way more than you do. What is it?

A: Your name.

Q: Two mothers and two daughters go fishing. Each of them catches ONE fish, for a total of THREE fish. How is this possible?

A: There was one mother, her daughter, and her daughter's daughter. This equals two mothers and two daughters . . . but only THREE people!

Q: How many times can you subtract 3 from 15?

A: Just once, and then it's not 15 anymore.

Q: No man wants to have this. But once he has it, no man wants to lose it. What is it?

A: A bald head.

Q: When you have this, you feel like sharing it. But if you do, you don't have it anymore. What is it?

A: A secret.

Q: One person can hold one.
Two people can share one.
But with three people, it disappears entirely.
What is it?

A: It's still a secret!

Q: What's the difference between an old dime and a new penny?

A: Nine cents.

Q: A man kills his brother in front of many witnesses, including reporters and police officers. Even so, he'll never be charged with a crime. Why?

A: He was an executioner, and his brother had been sentenced to death. (*Yeesh!*)

Q: On a football team, which player wears the biggest helmet?

A: The one with the biggest head.

Q: A cowgirl rode into town on Friday. She stayed one night, and then rode out again on Friday. How is this possible?

A: Her horse is named Friday.

Q: It was a terrible storm, but the man caught in it didn't get wet at all. How come?

A: It was a sandstorm.

Q: What's the difference between a toilet and a chair?

A: If you don't know, you're never coming to my house again!

Q: A family has five sisters, and each sister has one brother. How many kids are in the family?

A: Six. Each of the five sisters has only one brother. Add that one brother to the five sisters, and you have six.

Q: It has cities but you can't live in them.
It has oceans but there's no swimming.
It has forests but the trees can't be climbed.
What is it?
A: A map.

Wow, after all that laughter and thinking, we should probably stop now. But there is only ONE way to end this excellent chapter: with a turtle riddle!

Q: Imagine you're in a sinking canoe surrounded by starving alligator turtles. How can you survive this horrible fate?
A: Stop imagining.

HILARIOUS HOLIDAYS

The cool thing about holidays is that they don't come along every day. Er, hang on—strike that. Holidays DO come along every day. Apparently, there is nothing unusual about them at all. Rats![1]

Ooh, I have a special offer! Anyone who celebrates all of the holidays in this chapter is eligible to win a free car![2] So get on over to the party store and get ready to celebrate Blame Someone Else Day. This wonderful holiday is celebrated on the first Friday the 13th of the year. It could also be called Irresponsibility Day, because it's a time to celebrate all the

---

1. William Shakespeare once said, "If every day was a holiday, having fun would be as boring as work." (Those weren't quite his exact words.)
2. Of course, it's one thing to be *eligible* and another thing to actually win.

things you *didn't* do. (But be careful. If someone else finds out about this day, they just might be blaming YOU!)

JANUARY

I nternational Creativity Month, National Prune Breakfast Month, National Oatmeal Month, It's Okay to Be Different Month, and International "Get Over It" Month. Also includes "Someday We'll Laugh About This" Week and National Fresh-Squeezed Juice Week.

January 1: This day is in NO way special . . . except it *is* Get a Life Day. But that's it! Now move along, there's nothing to see here.

ATTACK OF THE GOBLINS!

From December 25 to January 6 are the Days of the Kallikantzaroi! The Kallikantzaroi are small Greek goblins who live underground most of the year. There they carbo-load on worms, snakes, and frogs. But starting on December 25, their annual aboveground funfest starts. But what's fun for a Greek goblin is un-fun for the rest of us. The goblins pee in flowerbeds, spoil food, tip things over, and break furniture.

Amazingly, the Kallikantzaroi are popular in Greece. People aren't frightened of them, since there are traditional and fun ways to keep the troublemakers away, like burning an old shoe. Awesome!

January 2: Run It Up the Flagpole and See If Anyone Salutes Day

January 3: Drinking Straw Day and Humiliation Day

January 4: Trivia Day

January 5: Great Fruitcake Toss. A day for tossing, hurling, and launching leftover fruitcakes! (Or at least it is in Manitou, Colorado.)

January 7: Rock Day and "I'm Not Going to Take It Anymore" Day

January 8: Bubble Bath Day and Women's Day in Greece. Women in Greece do absolutely no housework. Instead, they hang out in cafes and go shopping. Men are supposed to work in the home, vacuuming and cleaning. (And if they get caught outside, they may be drenched with water!)

January 10: Peculiar People Day

January 11: International Thank-You Day. Hey, do you know when International "You're Welcome" Day is? Neither do I. Thanks for nothing! (This is also Step in a Puddle and Splash Your Friend Day.)

January 13: International Skeptics Day. A good day to question EVERYTHING . . . including why there is a holiday for this!

January 14: Dress Up Your Pet Day. (Trust me, your goldfish will LOVE this.)

January 16: National Nothing Day

January 18: National Thesaurus Day and Winnie the Pooh Day. You got a problem with that?

January 20: Penguin Awareness Day

January 21: Squirrel Appreciation Day

January 22: Answer Your Cat's Question Day*

January 23: National Compliment Day and National Pie Day. Ooh, you could compliment someone's pie! Just make sure they understand what you mean when you say, "My, your crust is so elegant and dry." (Oh, this is also Measure Your Feet Day.)

January 25: Opposite Day

January 27: National Chocolate Cake Day and Thomas Crapper Day. Crapper was an Englishman who helped perfect the flushing toilet in the 1800s.

January 28: National Kazoo Day and Bubble Wrap Appreciation Day

January 29: National Corn Chip Day

January 30: National Inane Answering-Machine Message Day*. "Inane" means "senseless," so leave a message on your machine that makes no sense!

January 31: Backward Day. Thank goodness this is different from Opposite Day. Otherwise, the pressure would be too great!

* More information on starred holidays at www.wellcat.com

FEBRUARY

Return Shopping Carts to the Supermarket Month, Canned Foods Month, and National Snack Food Month. Also includes International Flirting Week, Get Paid to Shop Week, National Pancake Week, and International Friendship Week.

February 2: Groundhog Day. I've never understood this holiday. (Please don't explain it to me; I'm happier this way.)

February 3: Bean-Throwing Festival in Japan. Throw beans into the corners of houses to drive out evil spirits. (And remember to say, "Devils out, happiness in!" while you do it.) Hanging sardine heads from your doorway also gets the evil spirits to back off . . . along with most people you know.

February 4: Thank a Mailman Day

February 7: Love Your Robot Day

February 9: Toothache Day. The Toothache Fairy will take a swing at your jaw if you're not flossing properly. Underwear Day in Brazil!

February 11: Don't Cry Over Spilled Milk Day. Hey, since this is also Bun Day, maybe you can wipe up the spilled milk with your buns!

February 12: International Pancake Day and Darwin Day

February 13: Get a Different Name Day*

February 14: Ferris Wheel Day and International Quirkyalone Day

February 15: National Gum Drop Day

February 20: Battle of the Flowers. In southern France, a day to throw flowers at anyone you want!

February 22: World Thinking Day

February 24: *Fastelavn*. In Denmark, children get to poke their parents awake with decorated sticks. Nursery schools have events called *"Slå katten av tønnen"* ("knock the cat off the barrel"). Children hit a wooden barrel with a stick and try to knock a stuffed cat off the top!

February 26: For Pete's Sake Day*

February 27: No Brainer Day

February 28: Public Sleeping Day. (In other words, take a nap in a public place!)

MARCH

National Peanut Month, National Noodle Month, National Kidney Month, National Frozen Food Month, and Optimism Month. Also includes Celebrate Your Name Week, National Chocolate Chip Cookie Week, and National Procrastination Week.

March 1: National Pig Day

March 2: Babysitter Safety Day

March 3: I Want You to Be Happy Day

March 6: National Procrastination Day

EL COLACHO!

Spain's *El Colacho* festival is usually held every March in the town of Castrillo de Murcia. Dating back to 1620, the festival is designed to drive evil away from the town with baby jumping!

Jumping *over* babies, I mean.

Here's how it works. First, a parade focuses all the resident evil in Castrillo de Murcia's church. The townspeople accomplish this by having men dressed as devils (well-dressed devils!) gather there.

Meanwhile, a bunch of babies are laid down outside the church. Nooo!

On a signal, the devils run out of the church, jump over the babies, and then keep going. This removes all evil from both the infants and the town. (It's a symbolic thing.) An amazing side effect of all this is that the babies are instantly potty trained!

Not really. (That would be cool, though.)

March 8: Uppity Women Day

March 9: Backstabbers' Day

March 10: Middle Name Pride Day

March 13: Ear Muff Day

March 15: Dumbstruck Day

March 16: Everything You Do Is Right Day

March 17: Submarine Day

March 18: Forgive Mom & Dad Day

March 20: Extraterrestrials Abduction Day

March 22: International Goof-Off Day and Near Miss Day

March 25: International Waffle Day (aka *Våffeldagen* in Sweden)

March 26: Make Up Your Own Holiday Day*

March 26: Teacher's Day. In the Czech Republic, all teachers get gifts from their students. Impress your own teacher by celebrating this holiday, and see if it affects your grade!

March 28: Something on a Stick Day

March 29: Happy Day

March 30: I Am in Control Day

APRIL

APRIL 2ND: "PeaNut BuTTeR & JeLLy" DAY!

APRIL 17th: CHeeSeBALL DAY!

APRIL 24th: "PiG iN A BLANKeT" DAY!

National Humor Month, National Welding Month, International Twit Award Month, National Grilled Cheese Sandwich Month, National Smile Month, and National Twinkie Month. Also includes National Karaoke Week, Egg Salad Week, Dumb Week (celebrated in Greece), Wildlife Week, and National TV Turnoff Week.

The first Monday back at school after spring break isn't exactly a holiday—it's called Black Monday. The third Thursday of April is National High-Five Day, when people can freely exchange high-fives with anybody. The Monday after Easter is Dingus Day, which is pretty weird. April also has Cussing Day!

WHAT ARE THEY THROWING? (AND WHY DOES IT SMELL SO BAD?)

On the third Saturday in April, the World Cow Chip Throwing Championship Contest takes place in Beaver, Oklahoma. This competition involves people throwing pieces of dried cow poop! The tradition stems back to when Native Americans used dried buffalo chips to burn for fires. Later on, white settlers did the same thing, harvesting cow chips from their pastures to stockpile for the cold winter months. Whole families would go out to chuck cow pies into their wagons. It was a cow chip throwing frenzy!

Since 1970, it's also been a competition! But contestants have to be careful when throwing their cow poop. As the official chow chip throwing Web site says, "Wind velocity and direction play an important role."

April 1: National Hug Your Newsperson Day. In Scotland, they call this Huntigowk Day!

April 2: National Peanut Butter and Jelly Day

April 3: International Pillow Fight Day

April 4: Tell a Lie Day

April 7: No Housework Day*. If someone suggests you do some housework, quote the philosopher Baruch Spinoza: "Nature abhors a vacuum."

April 9: Name Yourself Day

April 10: National Siblings Day

April 12: International Teens Against Zits Day and Big Wind Day

April 14: International Moment of Laughter Day

April 15: Festival of the Sardine in Spain

April 17: Cheeseball Day and Children's Day. In Turkey, kids take over the government and get free ice cream and movies—all day!

April 18: International Jugglers Day

April 20: Look-Alike Day

April 21: Kindergarten Day

April 24: Pig in a Blanket Day

April 26: Hairball Awareness Day

April 30: National Sense of Smell Day and Hairstyle Appreciation Day

MAY

National "Get Happy" Month, More Than Just a Pretty Face Month, National Egg Month, Creative Beginnings Month, National Salsa Month, and National Hamburger Month. Also includes Be Kind to Animals Week and National Backyard Games Week.

The first Thursday of May is Space Day. Oh, and most important, National Digestive Disease Week is celebrated at the end of the month!

May 1: Save the Rhino Day

May 2: Brothers and Sisters Day (let's give a shout-out to our brothers and sisters!)

May 3: Hug Your Cat Day and Lumpy Rug Day

May 4: Kite Day

May 5: Unmothers Day, Slow Down Day, and Hoagie Day

May 6: No Homework Day*

May 8: Furry Day

May 9: Lost Sock Memorial Day

May 11: Twilight Zone Day

May 13: Frog Jumping Day

May 14: Dance Like a Chicken Day

May 16: Love a Tree Day and Sea Monkey Day

May 18: Mike the Headless Chicken Day

May 21: Other Mother's Day

May 23: World Turtle Day

May 24: National Escargot Day. Time to eat some snails!

May 25: National Tap Dance Day

JUNE

National Accordion Awareness Month, Aquarium Month, National Hermit Week, Frozen Yogurt Month, Candy Month, and National Pest Control Month. This is also the month the world celebrates International Pickle Week.

The first Friday in June is National Doughnut Day, and the first Saturday in June is Change Your Mind Day. World Juggling Day also bobbles around this month.

HOLLERIN' CONTEST DAY

This most excellent holiday is celebrated on the third Saturday in June. What makes it especially appealing is that it gives us a chance to scream and yell as loud as possible. No, I mean YELL! And try to find out who has the biggest leather lungs around. (But before you do this, you might want to warn the neighbors so they don't think someone's being murdered.).

If you're in the neighborhood, swing by Spivey's Corner in North Carolina. That's where the National Hollerin' Contest is held each year.

June 1: Dare Day, Flip a Coin Day, and International Child Protection Day. To celebrate Child Protection Day, babies compete in a crawling race in Lithuania. (Really.)

June 3: National Hug Your Cat Day

June 6: National Yo-Yo Day

June 8: Best Friends Day

June 9: Donald Duck Day

June 11: National Hug Day. The beauty of Hug Day is that after you get one hug, refills are free!

June 15: Smile Power Day

June 18: National Splurge Day and International Panic Day

June 19: World Sauntering Day

June 22: Mirthday!

June 24: Stalk Like a Ninja Day (*Yes!*)

June 26: Shrimp Festival Day. A day to celebrate seafood *and* short people.

June 27: Ferret Awareness Day and Leon Day. It is exactly six months until Christmas on Leon Day. ("Leon" is "Noel" spelled backward.)

June 29: Waffle Iron Day

JULY

ational Baked Bean Month, Cell Phone Courtesy Month, National Hot Dog Month, and Anti-Boredom Month! Also includes National Nude Recreation Week, Compliments Week, National Baby Food Week, Spam Festival Week, and Mosquito Week!

July 1: International Joke Day

July 2: I Forgot Day

July 4: Turtle Independence Day in Hawaii!

July 6: Nothing Day/National Pickle Festival

July 7: Father–Daughter Take a Walk Together Day

July 10: Don't Step on a Bee Day*

July 14: Pandemonium Day

July 15: Be a Dork Day.* Be a dork and be proud. Wave to squirrels, wear goofy clothes, and fall off a swing!

July 19: Cow Appreciation Day

July 20: World Jump Day. If at least six hundred million people in North and South America jump at the same time on this day, it will push the earth into a new orbit and help stop global warming! Also Ugly Truck Day.

July 21: National Ice Cream Day

July 23: "Hot Enough for Ya?" Day*

July 26: All or Nothing Day

July 27: Take Your Houseplants for a Walk Day*

July 31: Mutt's Day

AUGUST

Foot Health Month, Admit You're Happy Month, and National Catfish Month! Also includes International Clown Week, National Friendship Week, and National Smile Week.

The last Wednesday of August is the Festival of the Tomatoes (*Festival de la Tomatina*) in Buol, Spain. Over eight hundred thousand tomatoes are used in this colossal tomato fight. The streets run red to celebrate a time when a tomato cart was knocked over in the town, resulting in an argument and a tomato fight. Go figure!

August 2: National Ice Cream Sandwich Day

August 3: Watermelon Day

August 4: National Sisters' Day

August 5: National Mustard Day

August 6: Wiggle Your Toes Day and Fresh Breath Day

August 8: Sneak Some Zucchini on Your Neighbor's Porch Day*

August 9: Book Lover's Day and International Noogie-Givers' Day

August 10: Lazy Day. You'll need to save your energy for what's coming up August 15!

August 13: Left Handers Day

August 15: National Relaxation Day

August 16: National Tell a Joke Day. Please turn to page 143.

August 18: Bad Poetry Day*

August 22: National Punctuation Day

August 25: Kiss-and-Make-Up Day

August 26: Dog Day

August 27: Just Because Day

August 30: Frankenstein Day

SEPTEMBER

National Little League Month, National Mushroom Month, and National Literacy Month. Also includes Biscuits and Gravy Week, National Dog Week, and National Waffle Week.

The fourth Saturday of September is International Rabbit Day.

September 1: Knowledge Day (in Latvia)

September 2: Beheading Day

September 5: Be Late For Something Day

September 6: Read a Book Day and Do It Today Day

SEPTEMBER 28: ASK A STUPID QUESTION DAY!

What's the opposite of a camel? One expert says it's a soap dish. (It's not alive, it's found in moist places, and it has no hump.) If you think that was a stupid question, you're right! Stupid questions can take two forms:

1. A question you should already know the answer to. (Example: "What's my name?")

2. A question that's so silly, it never should have been asked at all. (Example: "Which is older: pencils or dirt?")

The Any Questions Answered (AQA) service collected some of its stupidest questions and then answered them gracefully. For example:

Q: What's the funniest word in the world?
A: The funniest word in the English language is *fartlek* (an athletic training regime); other funny words include *furphy*, *pratfall*, *parp*, and *firkin*.

Q: What is the best type of cookie to make a mattress from?
A: Fig or strawberry Newtons would be soft, but still provide some back support.

Q: I want to write a film script that makes me millions: what should it be about?
A: Your script should be about a young wizard and a robot looking for a ring on a pirate ship that sinks.

September 11: No News Is Good News Day

September 12: Destroy All Video Games Day

September 13: Fortune Cookie Day and Defy Superstition Day. So eat a cookie, read your fortune, and then crumple it up and defy it! (Unless it's a really good one!)

September 14: National Cream-Filled Doughnut Day

September 16: National Play-Doh Day and Collect Rocks Day

September 17: Apple Dumpling Day

September 19: Talk Like a Pirate Day

September 22: Elephant Appreciation Day

September 23: Checkers Day

September 24: Buy Nothing Day

September 25: National Comic Books Day

OCTOBER

National Toilet Tank Repair Month, Eat Ham Month, Sarcastic Month, National Pretzel Month, and, most important, the Month of the Hedgehog. Also includes National Pickled Pepper Week, National Pet Peeve Week, and Hug a Vending Machine Week.

The first Saturday in October is Frugal Fun Day, a time to have cheap fun.

October 4: National Taco Day and World Animal Day

October 7: World Smile Day

October 9: Moldy Cheese Day, Curious Events Day, and Leif Erikson Day in the US. Why does a Viking have an American holiday? When asked this question, American politician Sig Rogich said, "It's one of my favorite days. Leif never gets any credit for discovering America [in the year 1000]. It's all Columbus this, Columbus that." (Rogich then admitted he had no idea when Leif Erikson Day is!)

October 12: Moment of Frustration Scream Day*

October 13: Skeptics' Day

October 14: Be Bald and Be Free Day*

October 15: National Grouch Day

October 18: No Beard Day

October 21: Babbling Day

October 24: National Bologna Day. *Yes!*

October 25: Sour Day and Punk-for-a-Day Day

October 26: The Most Unproductive Day in the World

October 29: Laugh Suddenly For No Reason A Lot Today Day

October 31: National Knock-Knock Day. (Please turn to page 147.) Wait, this is also Halloween? If you end up handing out any candy, put it inside a dry spittoon. Also known as a *cuspidor*, this will add the perfect element of grossness to a grisly evening! Oh, and if you get to wear a costume to school, try dressing as one of your teachers. This is (almost) always funny!

WARNING: Ninety percent of parents admit they steal candy from their kids' bags. (The other 10 percent lie.) So keep an eye on 'em!

NOVEMBER

NOVEMBER 2ND: DEVILED EGG DAY!

NOVEMBER 6TH: "DO TATER TOTS EVER GROW UP" DAY!

NOVEMBER 28TH: FRENCH TOAST DAY!

Peanut Butter Lover's Month, Slaughter Month, and International Drum Month! Also includes National Split Pea Soup Week, National Fig Week, and National Make Up Your Own Week Week!

The Wednesday before Thanksgiving is Complaint-Free Wednesday, and the day after Thanksgiving is the National Day of Listening.

November 1: Vinegar Day

November 2: National Deviled Egg Day

November 3: Cliché Day

ANY TIME, ANY MONTH: THANKSGIVINGS!

The Thanksgiving tradition really did start with the Puritans who settled in New England. But here's the thing: the Puritans celebrated *Thanksgivings*: plural! Anytime something really good happened ("The pirates are gone!"), it was time to have a festival and give thanks.

So how many Thanksgivings did the Puritans celebrate? Sometimes as many as nine a year! So don't get stuck on that same old idea of having Thanksgiving only once a year. The next time something good happens ("The ninjas are gone!"), break out the gravy and pumpkin pie! (What? Don't you eat it that way, too?)

November 4: Chair Day/Mischief Night

November 5: Gunpowder Day

November 6: "Do Tater Tots Ever Grow Up?" Day

November 8: Dunce Day

November 9: Chaos Never Dies Day

November 11: Corduroy Appreciation Day

November 17: Take a Hike Day

November 18: International Science-Fiction Book Reshelving Day

November 19: Have a Bad Day Day*

November 20: Absurdity Day

November 21: False Confession Day

November 22: Start Your Own Country Day

November 28: National French Toast Day

November 29: Sinkie Day. (A "sinkie" is anyone who grabs a food item and then eats it over the sink.)

DECEMBER

R ead a New Book Month. Also includes National Hand-Washing Awareness Week. Oh, and the Festival of Zappadan is from December 4 to December 21.

December 1: Shavlik Randolph Day! Known to hoops fans as the finest player never to star in the NBA, Shavlik Randolph innovated the use of the "air five." (It's like a high-five with no hand contact.)

DECEMBER 5: KRAMPUSZ DAY

He's incredibly ugly. He's seven feet tall and carries a stick to frighten naughty children. But worst of all, his name is *Krampusz!*[3]

Krampusz is definitely the scariest mascot the Yuletide season has ever seen. He looks like a hairy giant with a goat's head. *Ulp.* For eight hundred years, Austrians have dressed up as Krampusz on this day. Then they go around the neighborhood knocking on doors. If children answer, the Krampusz is supposed to ring cowbells and scare the kids enough to make them REALLY look forward to the arrival of Saint Nicholas.

In the town of Schladming, there is a parade of over a thousand people dressed as Krampusz. The parade includes lots of revelry and cowbells (*yes!*). As they say in Austria: *"Krampusz gerne Partei"* ("Krampusz likes to party"). Remember, if you hear cowbells, don't answer your door!

3. From the old German word *krampen:* "claw"

December 2: Fritters Day

December 4: Wear Brown Shoes Day

December 5: Bathtub Party Day

December 6: Gazpacho Day

December 9: Boring Celebrities Day

December 16: National Chocolate-Covered Anything Day

December 20: Underdog Day

December 21: Humbug Day* and Flashlight Day

December 23: Night of the Radishes and Festivus! Festivus was intended to be a holiday that requires no shopping. The only Festivus decoration is a bare metal pole, which can be stuck in a pot or hung from the ceiling. (Because the pole is bare, one of the mottos for Festivus is "It's time to decorate the pole! We're done!") Festivus is a time to complain about important things. The holiday should also include feats of strength; as a matter of fact, Festivus is not over until the head of the household is wrestled to the ground and pinned.

December 26: National Whiner's Day

December 28: Card Playing Day

December 31: National Make-Up-Your-Mind Day, Unlucky Day, and You're All Done Day

FUN WITH FOOD

I used to think food was overrated. But then I went three hours without eating anything, and I nearly starved to death! Luckily, a nice lady gave me a rutabaga to gnaw on. That was NOT fun. (Memo to self: pack a lunch the next time you go to the roller-skating rink.)

Speaking of lunch, I like to pack mine in a bento box. That way, everything's organized in its own little compartment. Which is weird, because I'm usually the least organized person around—look, I just found an old cookie on my desk! Wow, it's stale but (like *all* cookies) edible.[1]

1. *nom nom nom*

Today, I have a new respect for food. Not only does it often taste good, but as this chapter will show, sometimes you can have fun *without* eating it! Now, I should point out that I eat a very healthy diet. Yep, fruits and vegetables at every meal. (Seriously.) But when I was thinking of *fun* foods, one of the first things to come to mind was a doughnut.

Even its name is fun: *doughnut.*

Back in the 1500s, a genius baker in Holland invented the first doughnut. It didn't have a hole; those didn't appear for another couple hundred years. The Dutch called this pioneer doughnut an *olykoek*: "oily cake."

Oily cake?

That sort of takes the fun out of it, doesn't it?

RANDOM FOOD FUN!

When sitting down to eat with a group, give your plate a serious look and quietly say, "I'm going to eat lightning and then poop thunder." Then start eating.

Bonus score if you look up after a few bites and say, "What?"

OCTOPUS FOOD!

Eight-Legged Banana: This is a real hit with kids who enjoy eating bananas and/or cephalopods.

1. Get a banana.

2. As you break the stem of the banana to begin peeling it, try to divide the peel into four roughly equal arms. Peel these about halfway down the banana.

3. Break off the exposed half of the banana fruit.

4. Using food scissors or a sharp knife (careful!), cut each "arm" of the peel in half lengthwise. (This should give the peel eight arms.)

5. Turn the banana so that the arms support it and the unpeeled half is vertical. If you want to get fancy, cut two slits in the vertical peel where the octopus's "eyes" would be. Stick raisins in there.

6. Slice up the broken half of the banana and garnish the plate with them. Serve.

★ Just wondering: If vitamin A helps with my sense of sight, what vitamin will enhance my Spidey sense?

Octopus Hot Dogs: *Question*: What do a boiling hot dog and an octopus have in common? *Answer*: They're both aquatic invertebrates. (Wow, that's not even a joke!)

1. Boil a hot dog. Remove from water and let cool.

2. Take a knife and make a crosscut at the end of the hot dog. Carefully cut down about two-thirds of the hot dog. This should give you four arms.

3. Carefully cut each arm in half, giving you eight arms.

4. Use your knife to cut little eyeholes where the octopus's head would be. Stuff onion, pickle relish, mustard, or sauerkraut in there. Serve.

5. I almost forgot! Get some wiener forks from a store that has unusual cutlery. Why? Because I  have decided that "wiener fork" is the greatest phrase in the English language. ("Who wants a wiener fork?" "Pass this wiener fork down the table, please.")

BREAKFAST BAG

This is a good meal to eat when you're out camping in the wilderness or spending the night at a friend's house and all they have to eat is a plastic yodeling pickle. But before you prepare it in those faraway places, practice it once at home.

First, you need some zip-lock freezer bags. These are handy because you can put them in boiling water—and that's just what you're going to do! But first you have to put some food in the bag. Start out like you're going to make some scrambled eggs. I do this by cracking two or three eggs into a bowl, adding a splash of milk, and then whisking them up. But instead of pouring this mix into a pan, for the Breakfast Bag, you pour it into the zip-lock bag! Then zip the bag shut and drop it into a big pot of boiling water.

Weird, huh? Have some tongs nearby, and make sure the bag doesn't drape over the edge of the pot or it will melt. You want to keep the bag in the water. Keep an eye on it, and when it looks done, it is. Then just "tong" the bag out, pour the eggs on a plate, and enjoy!

EGG FUN!

If you have leftover eggs in the fridge, get a marker and draw some faces on them! (And don't tell anyone it was you.)

PRETZEL LOGIC

I think pretzels are fun, and here's why: they're sort of tasty, and they have an interesting shape.

Hmmm, that's a pretty weak argument.

Okay, how about this: fun-loving kids helped invent them! About 1,400 years ago, the famous ruler Charlemagne made it a law that bakers had to make bread that included the shape of a cross. (Charlemagne was a Christian.) So at first, bakers just made their loaves the usual way, but then they rolled two "snakes" of dough and crossed them on top of the loaves.

But kids liked to pull the cross off and eat it, so the bakers started making the cross by itself and then rolling a circle around it so that it held together. One of these was called a *pretiola*, or "little reward." (The *pretiola* came to be known as a reward for kids, and from that came the pretzel!)

CAKE FUN!

Did you know there's an unusual European dessert known as "spit cake"? It's a tall, narrow cake that is made on a spinning rotisserie, which is known as a "spit." (What, you didn't think they put saliva in it, did you?)

EATING WITH YOUR HANDS

I have two possibilities for good finger food. First up, Kentucky Fried Fingers! Actually, they're not fried—you bake or boil them. Just get some sausages and sliced almonds. Cook the sausages, and after they've cooled a bit, jam an almond into the end of each one so that they look like fingernails. *Ha!*

The next recipe, the Hand of Meat Loaf, is a little more complex. I'm going to assume you know how to make meat loaf. (If you don't, it's easy, and there's someone at home who can help you.) The beauty of meat loaf is that you can shape it into anything you want. The fact that people always shape meat loaf into something as boring as a *loaf* has always disappointed me.

So, you're going to make a meat loaf shaped like a big hand! The problem will be that the fingers will be so skinny, they'll want to detach from the palm of the meat loaf. To prevent this from happening, make your hand with webbed fingers. In other words, the fingers can be spread out a bit to look like a hand, but they should all be attached to each other. There should be a little bit of meat between the fingers.

For fingernails, put cut pieces of onion on the ends of the fingers. If your family cooks meat loaf with some sauce or cheese on top of the loaf, feel free to do that. (Covering the loaf with ketchup before baking will also work.) But leave the sauce off the fingernails.

For the final touch, freak out your meat loaf eaters with a punch that has a human hand floating in it! Just fill a rubber glove with any colored fruit drink. Put a rubber band around the end of the glove and then put it in the freezer. After the glove is frozen (and the punch is made), run some warm water over the glove and then pull it off the ice hand. And into the punch the hand goes!

FUN COMES IN ALL FLAVORS.

If you're ever in Smithfield, Virginia, don't forget to pay a visit to the world's oldest ham. It dates back to 1902. People line up to see it!

CHEESY ADJECTIVES!

I love cheese. And I love going into cheese shops. The finest cheese shop in New York City is called Murray's. When people visit, they are amazed at all the different types of cheese there are. So to help people *talk* about cheese, Murray's provides a handout with useful words!

The beauty of Murray's cheese list is that you can also use it to describe your friends. In fact, I just did this, and it made me laugh so hard, I dropped my cheese!

Looks: smooth, snowy, rindless, bright white, fluffy, furry, brown mottling, blackish, straw-colored, shiny, orange, rough, moldy, cloth-bound, craggy, glossy, pudgy, punctured, waxy, veined

Smell: citrus, milky, hay, ammoniated, stinky, barnyardy, pungent, bodily, wet dirt, straw, nutty, grassy, herbal, leathery, fruity, wet stone, mushroomy, earthy, cave

Flavor: peppery, milky, lactic, tangy, lemony, mushroomy, buttery, milky, bacony, fruity, meaty, salty, grassy, earthy, dates, hazelnuts, caramelized onions, butterscotch, metallic

Feeling: dry, dense, thick, creamy, pliable, runny, bulging, curdy, firm, elastic, hard, flaky, oozing, soft, high moisture

MAKE YOUR OWN CURDS? YES WHEY!

To make your own tasty cheese, all you need is some milk, plus some lemon juice, a thermometer you can stick into a hot liquid, and some cotton fabric called *muslin*.

Pour some water into a large pan and then place a bowl into the water. (The bowl should be one that can get hot, and its sides should stick ABOVE the waterline.) Put the pan on a stove on high or medium heat. As the water starts to bubble, pour a pint of milk into the bowl.

As the milk warms, check it with the thermometer to see when it reaches 100 degrees Fahrenheit. Once it does, turn off the stove and carefully take the bowl out of the pan.

Add some lemon juice to the milk. Stir the whole concoction, and you'll see the milk start turning into curds. (The curds are the chunks; the whey is the watery liquid left behind.) Add more lemon juice if this isn't happening! Then leave the mix alone for fifteen minutes.

While you're waiting, line a colander or sieve with the muslin. After the fifteen minutes are up, dump your cheese mix into the muslin and then tie the corners together. You have a cheese ball!

You need to let the cheese ball drain in the colander or leave it hanging over the edge of the sink for an hour before it'll be ready. Once the cheese is dry, get out some bread or crackers. Then unwrap the cheese, add whatever you want for flavor (herbs, salt, pepper), and have at it!

MOM, THE CHEESE IS SCARING ME!

Once upon a time, there was a common English cheese known as "Suffolk cheese." It was a REALLY hard, smelly, and horrible cheese. Sailors took Suffolk cheese out to sea because the stuff lasted forever. This cheese could never go bad because it already WAS bad! Plus, if you ever lost your anchor, you could just tie a chain around a block of Suffolk, and that would probably be a good replacement.

How bad was this cheese? Well, the saying went that Suffolk cheese was so scary and inedible, "pigs would grunt at it, dogs would bark at it, but none dared bite it." Wow!

OATMEAL CANNONBALL

There's a good reason to eat oatmeal: the empty cardboard container makes a perfect air cannon! Just cut a hole in the bottom end of the container big enough to fit your finger. Then get a rubber band and a large balloon. Stretch the balloon across the open end of the container and wrap the rubber band around its edges. Now pinch the skin of the balloon, pull it back, and let go! Out the other end of the oatmeal container will come an air cannonball. Even

though the cannonball is invisible, it will shoot across a
room, table, or countertop, amazing onlookers . . . just before
it blows them away!

HOW TO SURVIVE A FOOD FIGHT

I clearly remember the day I was sitting quietly in the
school cafeteria, playing with my Jell-O, when suddenly a
burrito went flying by my ear. Someone yelled, "Food fight!"
and then the air was filled with milk cartons, pizza crusts,
and doughnuts! Every single food item in the room was
catapulted into the air.

That was surprising. It was even more surprising when a
quesadilla flew through the air like a Frisbee and landed on
my head . . . with the melted-cheese side *down*. Rats!

Afterward, as I tried to pull the melted cheese out of
my hair, I thought about why people have food fights.

Sometimes these are just one-on-one battles, like when the gladiators of ancient Rome warily circled one another with banana cream pies. (If people in the Colosseum stuck out their thumbs, it meant they wanted to taste the pie.) And sometimes, as in the cafeteria, a food fight can be an unplanned, chaotic free-for-all.

If you get in a food fight, remember to never, ever throw an item that might hurt someone. The Jell-O on my plate would have been a good choice, but the giant pineapple I had in my lunch bag? Bad call. Throwing hot chocolate in someone's face is obviously a horrible idea. But don't bother throwing food that's *completely* harmless. If you're flinging pieces of popcorn at someone armed with a bologna-and-pickle sandwich, you're in trouble. Big trouble.

When considering what food items to throw, consider these factors:

★ Throwability: How easy will it be to chuck this item? Sure, spaghetti would be a cool food to throw, but it's not really practical to grab a handful of pasta. More of it will get on you than on your target! Likewise, anyone armed with a salad is at a disadvantage.

★ Stain Ethics: If you're throwing liquids, water and even milk aren't going to cause permanent stains on someone's clothes. Grape or blueberry juice, however, are brutal!

★ **Creativity:** Think outside the bento box! Is there a large spoon nearby that you could use to launch some mashed potatoes? And what about a squeeze bottle of mustard or ketchup? I bet that could fire a good stream!

★ **Explosiveness:** The perfect item should offer a combination of throwability and explosiveness. A raw egg has terrific explosiveness, but it would be too hard to hit someone with. (And that's why hard-boiled eggs are out of the question.) Ooh, I have it! A calzone has a crust around it, but if thrown with enough force, it might break open and reveal its meat and tomato filling!

Finally, remember that you always need to have an exit strategy. If you think a food fight is about to break out, stay away from the middle of any room. Also, don't sit with your back to anyone. Once the food starts flying, remember the motto of the hyperactive kid with a Scotch tape roll who sat next to me in first grade: "Stick and move, stick and move."

COOLEST SENTENCE OF THE CENTURY!

In 2004, a group of politicians in Taiwan sat down to have lunch together. It didn't go very well, as an argument led to a massive food fight! Afterward, one food-covered politician shouted, "My whole body smells like a lunch box!" Yes!

PAN CON TOMATE

Although a lot of the recipes in this chapter are more for fun than for food, I wanted to include one meal recipe that is simple and absolutely tasty. You might think from the heading that it's fancy. But the Spanish just translates to "bread with tomato," and as you'll see, that's almost all you need.

Ingredients:

> A good, juicy, ripe tomato
> Bread
> Olive oil
> Salt
> *Optional:* Garlic

First, toast the bread. Then get a bowl and start grating the tomato over the bowl. Discard the tomato skin as it gets torn off.

Put the toasted bread on a plate and drizzle some olive oil on it. (If you have garlic, put it on the bread before you add the olive oil.) Then get a spoon and scoop some tomato on the bread. Sprinkle a little salt on it, and you're done. Think of *pan con tomate* as a quick, healthy pizza. If you want cheese, sprinkle some Parmesan on top!

VEGGIE PHOBIA!

A person suffering from *lachanophobia* suffers horrible dread upon seeing a head of cauliflower. That's because *lachanophobia* is the fear of vegetables! (So if anyone ever hands you a plate of flaccid Brussels sprouts or limp lima beans, pretend you're a *lachanophobe*!)

EEEKKK!!

What? What?

IN AN EATING CONTEST? READ THIS!

I've never thought of professional eating contests as being all that fun. I mean, do I really want to see a guy shove sixty hot dogs into his mouth? Hmmm, maybe! But he'll also be soaking sixty hot dog buns in water and eating their soggy remnants. *Blech!*

However, *amateur* eating contests can be fun, if you follow these steps. First, don't choke. Seriously! I've choked on food when I wasn't even IN a contest . . . I was just *hungry!* To avoid choking, breathe through your nose the whole time you're eating. This will help keep things simple: air to your lungs, food to your stomach.

Also, never have an eating contest with a hard–to-chew item. Meat? No! Bread? Forget about it! And certainly no bread-and-meat combinations—that's just asking for trouble! Instead, stick to soft things like cake, pie, oatmeal, or meatballs.

Try to avoid taking big bites. The key to eating safely and fast is to take lots of small bites, chewing quickly and swallowing often.

Finally, never take part in more than one eating contest a year, because more than that is just unhealthy. Happy chewing to you, and break a leg! (But not a tooth.)

AMAZING MAZES

I once took two kids named Evan and Alaina to a giant cornfield maze. It was going to be fun, as long as we stuck together. This maze was really huge and complex.

Handing each kid a map, I said, "This will be fun, as long as we stick together. This maze is really huge and complex—"

"I like mazes!" shouted Evan. And with that, he ran into the maze entrance, his map fluttering to the ground behind him.

Sighing, I trudged alongside Alaina, and together we entered the maze. We were immediately hemmed in by tall cornstalks. As we moved through the maze, we checked every turn and dead end to see if Evan had gotten himself trapped. It took forever, but finally we emerged at the exit of the cornfield—and we *still* hadn't found him!

We decided to wait for Evan to come out. He had to be in there somewhere! Sure enough, twenty minutes later, the little corn sprite stepped out of the stalks with a smile on his lips.

"That was awesome!" Evan said.

He was having so much fun, I didn't have the heart to get angry. "Yeah," I said, "but you're supposed to—"

"Let's do it again, *backward!*" he yelled. Despite our shouted cries, Evan plunged back into the maze, leaving me holding out a map.

And if I blinked back a tear at that moment, I'll never tell.

· A BAD SIGN!

If you see a sign for a cornfield maze that says anything like "What a Maize!" or "It's Amaizing!" be sure to complain to the proper authorities.

The popularity of corn mazes is fairly recent. The beauty of them is that you can plant, create, and destroy them in just a few months. But the old-school version of these mazes came

HOW TO GET OUT OF A MAZE IN FOUR EASY STEPS!

1. Don't bother with trailing a ball of string or leaving bread crumbs behind you. This never actually works. Other people will just trip on the string. (And really small people will trip on the bread crumbs.)

2. The Golden Rule: Consistently turn left (or right) every time you come to an intersection. That way, you may go down some dead ends, but you'll probably get out of the maze just fine. (Hey, look out for that bread crumb!)

3. If you're in a really complex maze, the Golden Rule won't necessarily work because some parts of the maze won't be connected to outer walls. So I guess Rule 2 isn't really that golden after all.

4. Don't panic! You probably won't die, or even suffer, if you get stuck in the maze for a while. (Probably!) And trust me, there's nothing more pitiful than the person who comes lurching through the cornstalk wall of a maze with a scared expression. What are you going to say to the semi-disgusted people out there? "I panicked"? Take it from me, that's not going to impress them.

To prevent this embarrassment, get a map for your maze and put it in your pocket. Then if you get lost, pull out the map . . . only to realize that you have no idea *where* in the map you are! Then remember that you brought a compass. (You did bring a compass, right?) If not, *then* panic.

about in the 1500s. At that time, gardeners began laying out hedges in patterns that would more or less stay put for decades, and even centuries. The idea behind these "puzzle mazes" was that you could exercise your mind AND body while going through them. And if that's not a fun idea, I don't know what is!

Before hedge mazes existed, there were *labyrinths*. The earliest examples of these were not actually mazes at all. First, you weren't hemmed in on your sides. You could see where you were and where you were going! In other words, a labyrinth didn't usually have a bunch of dead ends. Instead, as the path turned and twisted, all you had to do was stay on it and you'd eventually reach your goal (which *could* be a dead end!).

Have you ever heard the famous myth of the Minotaur and the labyrinth? It's really about a monster that lived in the center of a *maze*, not a labyrinth. I know this because in the story, there's a big deal made about how the hero, Theseus, manages to figure out a way through the labyrinth to kill the monster, rescue the girl, and escape.

But if the Minotaur was hiding in a *labyrinth,* ANY applehead could have gotten to it!

It's easy to create your own labyrinth. Just follow these handy instructions! First, you just need to draw a cross. Then draw an "L" shape in each corner, and stick a dot in the middle of each one.

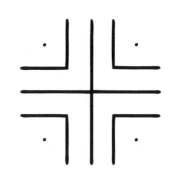

Now draw a loop from the top of the cross to the top of the "L" to its right. Then, as the illustration shows, move

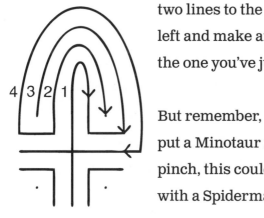

two lines to the left and make another, higher loop over the one you've just drawn. Keep going!

But remember, it's not final until you put a Minotaur in the center! (In a pinch, this could be the neighbor kid with a Spiderman mask.)

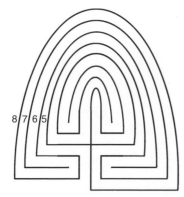

ENTER ↗

Once you start thinking about mazes, you'll see them everywhere. For example, I'm writing this as I walk in a downtown area, and this place is a TOTAL maze. All the intersecting streets, alleys, and dead ends—HEY!

I seem to have fallen down a manhole. (Are you impressed that I could keep writing even as I fell down the hole?)

And down here in the sewers is ANOTHER huge network of mazes. Stinky, stinky mazes. Every civilized city has a sewer maze beneath it, and some of these mazes are world famous. London's sewer has miles of unexplored tunnels. And Paris has an insane combination of sewers, quarries, and tombs known as the Catacombs buried under its streets. *Sacré p.u.!*

To give you an idea of how impressive the maze beneath Paris is, there is no map to it because it's so colossal. Experts

POOP IN A MAZE

guess that there are 124 miles of subway track, 185 miles of Catacombs, and 1,300 miles of sewer tunnels down there!

If you ever find yourself trapped in an underground maze, don't feel sorry for yourself. Lots of cultures believe bad luck can't follow a maze, and one traditional Chinese belief is that demons can only go in a straight line.

So you'll have that going for you.

Ooh, I just thought of...

The most fun you could ever have in a maze!

Go to a hedge maze or a cornfield maze. Learn its route pretty well. Then put on a bull mask (so you look like the Minotaur) and run through it making bellowing sounds!

★ Don't have a bull mask? Preferred substitutes include a gorilla mask, a hockey mask, and, of course, a Spiderman mask.

PLAYING GAMES

Did you know there's a National Toy Hall of Fame? Well, there is, and I just learned that "the ball" has been inducted into it. Want to know how many toys got inducted *before* the ball? Forty! What an outrage! Can you believe that things like the *cardboard box* (class of 2005) and the *stick* (class of 2008) got in before the ball?

Man, I'm so mad right now! Luckily, this wonderful joke put me back in a good mood.

Q: What's brown and sticky?

A: A stick.[1]

1. If you thought "dung" was the punch line, *please.* That's the answer to the question, "What's brown and sounds like a bell?"

Anyway, many of the best games involve a lot of people. That way, everyone can share the fun! For example, if you're at the pool with three or more people, have a Nose-Nudge Relay. It's a swimming race from one side of the pool to the other, but don't worry if you're not a fast swimmer. This isn't just any old race!

In the Nose-Nudge Relay, you have to use your nose to nudge a Ping-Pong ball across the pool! This is both very fun and surprisingly funny. If you don't have enough Ping-Pong balls, you can just pour a little water into a balloon and then blow up the balloon and tie off the end.

If you don't have a swimming pool in the next room, please turn to page 53 of your history book. There you will see that explorer and writer Richard Burton (1821–1890) wrote a list of all sorts of fun things to do, including "cards, dice, shovelboard, chess, the philosopher's game, small trunks, shuttlecock, billiards, music, masks, singing, dancing, frolics, jests, riddles, catches, questions and commands, and merry tales of errant knights, queens, lovers, lords, ladies, giants, dwarfs, thieves, cheaters, witches, fairies, goblins, and friars."

So go enjoy a rousing match of shovelboard, and then tell the story of an errant friar. It'll be AWESOME!

★ What is a cannibal's favorite game?[2]

2. Swallow the leader.

BOO!

This awesome game is played after dark in a house you are familiar with. One person hides while all the others count loudly in one room. The person hiding has a good flashlight and hides somewhere where they can jump out and scare the pants off the group. The more searchers there are, the better. (They'll all end up piled together, saying, "I'm not looking in there, *you* look in there!")

It's ridiculous just how scary this whole thing is: You are in a familiar house, searching for someone you know, and *knowing* he or she will try to scare you. But somehow everyone will still jump out of their skin when the hider finally yells "Boo!" and turns the flashlight on their face.

HIDE IT AND THEY SEEK!

Little kids like to play hide-and-seek, but if you hide, they might just grab some car keys and take off. To prevent this from happening, wind up a kitchen timer and hide it. Then watch the kids try to find the ticking sound!

COIN HOOPS

This is a two-player event. You need at least one coin to play.

1. Flip a coin to see who goes first.

2. Sit facing each other across the table. The winner of the toss spins a coin on the table in front of her and then traps the spinning coin between her two thumbs.

3. The opposing player now sets the bottom edge of his palms on the table, pushes the tips of his fingers together, and then touches his thumbs so that he makes a "basket."

4. The player with the coin also sets her palms on the table (so that the fingertips touch). She still has the coin between her thumbs. She then swivels her thumbs upward so that the coin flicks forward and (hopefully) makes a basket!

5. Players alternate taking shots until a certain score is reached. The winner can be awarded all, some, or none of the coins depending on what the players agree on. (If no agreement is reached, both players keep their coins.)

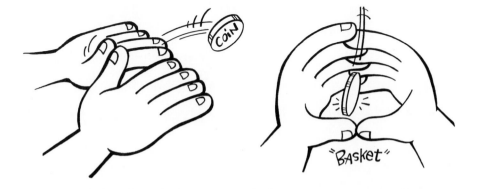

BOUNCY-BOUNCY!

If you have a variety of bouncing balls, try this: Take the larger of two balls (like a basketball) and perch another ball (like a Ping-Pong ball) on top of it. Then drop the stacked balls and stand back in amazement! You'll be surprised at how high the top ball bounces, while the bottom ball hardly goes anywhere! Try other ball duos, like a Super Ball on a volleyball or a tennis ball on a soccer ball, to discover the highest-bouncing combination.

★ Super-Insane Bouncy-Bouncy! If you do this trick, but substitute an egg for the small ball, the egg will fly far away. (So don't do it indoors!)

BFF CARRYING

Have you ever heard of the Wife-Carrying World Championship? It's held every year in Finland. Men try to set speed records as they run through obstacle courses while carrying their wives. At least that's how I *thought* it worked! After training for hours, my wife and I flew to Finland and discovered this in the rule book: *"The wife to be carried may be your own, the neighbor's, or you may have found her farther afield."*

Did you see that? Contestants don't even have to carry their own wives! Sheesh. But one thing I like about the competition is that it encourages teamwork and sportsmanship. This is something that the famous Italian painter Caravaggio (1571–1610) never learned. He was playing tennis when an argument about the score led him to murder his opponent. (I'm guessing the score did not include the word "Love.")

To honor the Wife-Carrying World Championship, come up with your own variation: BFF Carrying! All you need to do is this:

1. Set up an obstacle course

2. Get some competitors who have best friends they can carry.

3. Start running the BFFs through the course!

OBSTACLE COURSES!

Have you ever wondered who invented the first obstacle course? Well, I'm a historian, and I believe it was an unnamed girl in the Middle Ages who wanted a Popsicle. But to get to the Popsicle shop, this girl had to jump over a puddle, run from a mean dog, climb a castle wall, and then swing from a vine into the shop window. (That's how hard it was to get a Popsicle back then!)

And as this medieval girl enjoyed her hard-won 'sicle, she thought, "That was fun!"

She told her village friends about the adventure. It sounded like something they should all try! Soon, the shop was invaded by kids swinging through the windows. And after that, these kids invented new obstacle courses that involved hopping on one leg, crawling, swimming, horseback riding, skateboarding, scooting, scootering, and running from enraged knights.

Try setting up an obstacle course in your backyard or at the park with boxes, lawn chairs, and cones. For variety, try to have objects that you go over, through, under, and around. For example, you could tie off a rope for players to jump *over*, then have an open cardboard box or old tire to go *through*. Next, have a rug for people to go *under*, and then plant a tree for them to go *around*!

Remember, variety is everything. Where the racers want to sprint around the tree, you could make that the crabwalk portion of the course! (Or the "walking backward" portion, or any other goofy thing you want!)

To slow things down, try having a balance beam somewhere on the course that contestants have to walk across. If they fall off the beam, they have to go back to the beginning and try again! And laying a ladder down on the ground makes a good obstacle to scamper through. (But don't use this with little kids, because they might trip.)

Lastly, have a good final obstacle. The coolest one would pay tribute to the original inventor of the obstacle course by having a rope swing that ends with a splash into a kiddie pool!

★ The only obstacle course I don't like is an ice-skating obstacle course. This is probably because I almost broke my neck doing one. (Why did I think I could jump OVER that barrel?)

MORE CREATIVE IDEAS!

Have contestants . . .

roll their bodies along the top of big exercise balls for ten yards.

step on a balloon and pop it before continuing through the course.

answer a Game Show Host who asks odd questions like, "What's your brother's favorite color?" or "Have you ever stuck gum in your hair to see what would happen?"

swing from monkey bars for part of the course. (If no monkey bars are available, ape handles or lemur beams may be used instead.)

shoot a ball (give them three tries) to make a basket on a hoop that another kid is holding. If they make the shot, they can continue. (Or if they miss all three attempts, they still get to continue!)

eat a bowl of cereal or Jell-O quickly (or something else that they probably won't choke on).

ride a zip-line from a tree and into a giant bowl of cereal or Jell-O (or something else they won't drown in).

climb inside a giant hamster ball and roll it from the INSIDE.

OBSTACLE COURSE OF IMAGINATION!

an, there are so many good obstacle course ideas, my head is spinning. But the one thing all courses have in common is that contestants are timed to see who gets through fastest, right? **Wrong!**

In an Imaginary Obstacle Course, competitors probably won't make it through at all. That's because they will have to overcome obstacles like the Whirling Ninja, the Kiddie Pool of Death, and the Bottomless Pit, which are all pretty dangerous.

But luckily, they're also imaginary!

First, decide what imaginary obstacles you want your course to have. You may want to use a rock or branch or some other marker to show where you imagine an obstacle to be. As you walk through the course, draw a basic map showing where and what each obstacle is. (Example: "Here's where you have to walk a tightrope over burning coals. Then you have to crawl like a soldier. And then you have to pull the tail of the Snapping Turtle of Destruction. It may try to twirl around and bite you, so be careful!")

The key to running an Imaginary Obstacle Course is to do it where *other* people can see you. This might be in a park on a sunny day or near a field where a soccer game is underway. As your contestants go through your course, they may appear a little eccentric to any onlookers.[3] This is good! Half the fun of this obstacle course is how kooky it looks to outsiders.

3. Actually, they'll look insane.

Onlooker: "Why is that boy yelling and acting like he's being hacked by swords?"

You: "He tried to crawl between the legs of the Whirling Ninja . . . and failed."

Onlooker (*confused*): "Oh."

If you run into imaginary trouble doing this obstacle course (and you will!), don't worry. You don't have to finish! Plus, it might give you a chance to use lines like this:

★ "Go ahead . . . keep going . . . without me."

★ "I tried my best—*cough weakly*—but now I feel the Snapping Turtle's breath upon my brow."

★ "Tell Mom I love her. But don't tell my brother anything, because I can see him over there sticking his tongue out at me."

Choosing a winner isn't absolutely necessary with this course. But if you insist, the winner could be whoever does the most incredible acting job or whoever attracts the most onlookers while running the course. Or you could just say everyone is a winner, except anyone who actually finishes the course!

TUG OF PEACE?

Here's my theory: If you were stuck on a desert island, the best thing to have with you (besides food and water) might be a piece of rope! A rope is a good tool, plus you can practice your knots and even have games of tug-of-war with . . . yourself.

As you know, in a tug-of-war, the strongest, heaviest competitor usually wins. But this isn't necessarily the case with the game I want to describe: the tug-of-peace! It's played like tug-of-war, in that the contestants need a rope and a soft setting in case they fall down. (A lawn or even a thick carpet can work.) Where tug-of-peace is different is in the fact that competitors will be standing on something! Upside-down milk crates that are a foot tall or shorter are perfect for this. These should be set up no more than fifteen feet apart. Then the contestants stand on the crates and take hold of the rope. If the rope is rough, it's a good idea for the contestants to wear gloves so that they don't get rope burn.

On a signal, both tug-of-peace pullers try to pull the other person off the crate. But here's where a tricky person can beat a big one! Instead of pulling, one person might let the rope go slack. So when the other person pulls, suddenly there's no resistance and he falls off the crate!

KEEP THAT RALLY GOING!

The game of badminton has been around for a LONG time. In ancient Babylonia, there was a fortune-telling version of the game that used a ball. People believed that the amount of time the ball was kept in play was a way to tell how long the players would live.

But nobody called badminton "badminton" until there was a big tournament of the game held at a duke's country house in 1873. The place was known as "Badminton House," and the rest was history![4]

4. Hey, if you're good at *bad*minton, are you bad at *good*minton?

TOILET TAG

No game has ever combined the wonder of tag with the charms of plumbing—until now! (I think.)

To get started, select a player to be the Plumber. (If you have a large group, you may choose to have more than one Plumber.) While the other players scatter, the Plumber closes his eyes and counts to an arbitrary number. Upon reaching said number, the Plumber begins trying to tag other players.

When a player is tagged, he impersonates a toilet by kneeling on one knee and holding one arm out to the side. This player must stay frozen as a toilet until another player comes and sits on the his knee and pushes down on his arm while making a flushing sound. ("*Whoosh*" is a sensible choice.) This flushing unfreezes the toilet player, and both players are now free to escape the clutches of the Plumber. If a player is tagged twice by the Plumber, he or she also becomes a Plumber.

Play can continue until all players are frozen, or until a certain time limit is reached. The last player to be frozen or the last player left can be the Plumber for the next round.

THE NAME OF THE GAME!

If you've played bingo, it's possible you've used dry beans to cover your card. That's good, since the game was originally called Beano! A toy salesman named Edwin Lowe played this version with his family in the 1930s, but his young daughter would yell "Bean-go!" when she won. And as Lowe helped make the game more popular, he honored his daughter by changing the name of the game.

"SAVE A LIFE" RELAY

You don't have to do this as a relay race, but it's one possibility. Okay, first you need some Life Savers candy. Then get some plastic drinking straws. Now, for every two players, cut one straw in half. Give one of the cut straws to each person.

"But how many players do we need?" you ask. Good question! Keep reading this, and then you can decide for yourself.

Now the contestants line up. The person who will start the relay race puts her straw in her mouth. She then perches the Life Saver at the end of the straw. She turns to the next person in line behind her. This person also has a straw in his mouth! Working together, but without using their hands, the two contestants slide the Life Saver from the first straw to the second!

And so the relay race continues until the last person in line gets the Life Saver.

Note: If the Life Saver falls to the ground, try to save it before it gets all dirty. Put it back on the very first straw on the relay race. Alternatively, the person who drops the Life Saver has to eat it.

BUTTOCKS-POPPING RELAY

Although the title of this competition is unfortunate, it is like any relay race. Of course, you need people. And naturally, they come equipped with buttocks. But in this case, these should also be people who don't mind getting wet!

Oh, and you also need some water balloons.

Fill up half-again as many water balloons as you have people. In other words, if you have twenty people, you'll want to fill twenty balloons. Then take half of twenty (which is ten!) and fill up that many MORE balloons. These last ten are spares, and they're always good to have.

Once you're done with that, the tricky part of this race is that once you get a lot of water balloons around a bunch of kids, it's hard to resist the temptation to start throwing them at each other! To solve this problem, fill the water balloons and put them in a cooler or two. Place the coolers at the front of the relay racers' lines, along with a responsible person (preferably an adult).

As the front person in the line comes forward, the adult will hand him a water balloon. The front person has to run with the balloon to some marker (say, twenty yards away) and then sit on the water balloon to get it to pop! If the person makes a good effort and just can't get his butt to pop the balloon, he can try other means, like stomping on the balloon or verbally attacking it.

If the balloon pops while the runner is yet to get to the marker, he has to come back and get another one.

Note: Want to make it tougher to pop those balloons? Don't fill them so full!

HAVE SNOWBALLS? COMMENCE THROWING!

T here is a group known as the International Federation of Snowball Throwing (IFST). Its goal is to make snowball throwing an Olympic sport, and to keep things organized, its members have created "rules." Here are a few of them!

★ All snowballs must be hand-packed after the start of competition. Stockpiling snowballs in advance is a method used only by guerrilla-style snowball gangs.

★ There is not a regulated playing field for snowball throwing. Snow knows no boundaries, and neither do snowball throwers.

★ Teams do not have to have equal numbers of players.
There is not a minimum number of players for each
team. If you are overly confident in your snowball-
throwing abilities, you could agree to take on an entire
neighborhood. That's cool with us.

★ Competition ends when an individual or entire team runs
out of snowballs, declares defeat, or runs home to their
mommies, whichever happens first.

★ No throwing ice or yellow snow.

★ If a judge spots a player crying, that player is
automatically disqualified. There is no crying in snowball
throwing.

GOT MUD?

T he people of Germany have some cool games, like the
World Beard Championships and Plastic Duck Racing.
But let's concentrate on my favorite, the Mud Olympics!
These Olympic games involve regular sports like soccer,
volleyball, relay races, and even Ping-Pong. The only catch
is that they take place in the mud!

How do you play? You'll need some mud. If you're playing
Ping-Pong, it can just be enough mud to set up a table in.

Volleyball will take a little more room, and so forth. But whatever game you're playing, the goal is less to win and more to get totally covered in mucky muddy muddiness. If your soccer game or relay race is taking place in some good, deep mud, here's a bit of advice: Don't wear rubber boots! They'll just get stuck in the mud. The best choice is old tennis shoes wrapped with duct tape. Trust me! (And if you're going to play volleyball, use water balloons instead of balls. Hey, if the balloon pops, it will clean you off a little.)

NO HARM, NO FOUL WEATHER!

One fun game challenge is to agree to play certain outdoor games no matter the weather. For example, writer Ben Golliver said:

As a kid, my brother, neighbors and I would play basketball come rain or shine. Intense heat and snow were our two biggest problems. But during summers, when temperatures started really rising, we'd rig up a hose so that it would spray up into the air directly above the basketball hoop, causing a rain/mist effect over the court, allowing us to play for hours at a time without dying of heat stroke.

We termed this practice "Oregonian Basketball" because we were so used to playing in the rain. This was the pinnacle of fun!

But we never solved snow.

TABLETOP HOCKEY!

If mud is too . . . muddy for you, bring your sporting side back indoors. It's time to experience the majesty of tabletop hockey! Unlike real hockey, this game doesn't require much equipment. But you do need a table, a button (or other puck-like item) and two goals. One way to make two goals is to cut a plastic berry box in half. Flip the two halves upside down, and bingo! You're ready to hit the ice. (If you decide on making a penalty box, you're going to need a much bigger plastic berry box.)

SPORTING FUN!

Go to a sports event you wouldn't normally attend and have wholesome fan fun. Little League baseball, senior-citizen chess tournaments, and toddler marathons might be examples of sports where you can cheerlead like crazy and no one (usually!) minds. Just be *positive!* (For example, "Come on, number 32, you can do it!" "Checkmate him! You're the best!" and "I think I spilled my Coke. Yeah!")

THE JAR GAME

This Israeli game has sort of a boring name, so maybe I should call it by its original Hebrew title: תנצנצ קחשמה! (Does that help?) Anyway, you can play this game indoors or outdoors. To start, you need a big, wide-mouthed jar or container. Traditionally, each player also has a bag full of apricot pits. You may not want to eat dozens of apricots to get their pits, so get a bunch of small items that are like apricot pits. These could be unshelled walnuts, poker chips, peach pits—you name it.

Let's say the players are using walnuts. Each player puts three walnuts in the jar. Then each player stands at a distance of three to six feet from the jar. Decide on a distance and then don't let anyone's hand go over that line. (Some people may try to stretch toward the jar.)

The idea is that each player takes a turn trying to throw a walnut into the jar. If a player gets one in, she goes to the jar and takes two walnuts out! The game is over when the last walnut is taken. The players add up their walnuts and whoever has the most, wins.

The winner then gestures to the sky and cries out, "תנצנץ קחשממה‎!"

JUST GET THESE AWAY FROM ME!

A few years ago, Nike shot a "Just Do It" commercial in the African country of Kenya. The commercial featured members of the Samburu tribe. These folks wore Nike shoes and said things in their native tongue. Of course, no one from Nike spoke this language. And so it wasn't until after the ads went on the air that some people in the know heard a tribesman say, "I don't want these! I want big shoes!"

STICKBALL!

T he beauty of stickball is that it's a game you can play in the street. Empty parking lots and schoolyards also work. That means the playing field changes from street to street! To get started, you just need . . . wait for it . . . a stick and a ball. The stick could be a broom or mop handle, but anything similar can work. (A baseball bat will do, but it's too wide for most players.) To give your stick extra flair, spiral some duct tape around one half of it.

As for the ball, any small rubber ball works. Got a tennis ball? Great.

So, how do you play? It's sort of like baseball. You can have one to eight players to a team. And nobody uses mitts! You're going to need bases and a home plate, but since you might be in a street, these could be fire hydrants, steps, or manhole covers. (Note: Open manholes are not good choices.)

There are versions of stickball where a pitcher throws the ball to the batter. After one bounce, the batter takes a swing. If he misses, he usually only gets two strikes before he's out. Another fun version of stickball is Fungo. This is when the batter holds the ball with one hand and tosses it up in the air. Then he gets ready to hit it after it bounces once . . . or twice . . . or even three times!

How do you get an out? In addition to the usual ways (tagging the runner or throwing to a base on a forced out), players are out if the ball lands (and *stays*) on a porch, car, or the roof of anything. Oh, and if the ball breaks something? That's an out. And if that happens, you should either fix the broken thing or quietly quit playing. (Getting yelled at is definitely NOT fun.)

A PORTRAIT IN FUN!

Be brave! The time will come when, even with a book like this, fun will be in short supply. That's when it will be important to have a model of inspiration, a figure who can breathe life back into us and make us see the world for what it is: a very goofy place!

Mark Titus is just such a person. As a student at Ohio State University, he was the manager for the men's basketball team. His work wasn't very glamorous, as it involved doing things like filling water bottles for the players. But when the team lost some players, Titus was asked to join the roster. Awesome!

In his new role as benchwarmer, Titus was always the last player to be put into a game. But as a fun-loving person, that didn't matter! For instance, while he was waiting for a rare chance to be substituted into a game, there was a time-out on the floor. Titus ran back to the bench (without having played yet) and screamed, "Water! Water! I need water!"

Titus joked around all season, and in doing so, he showed that it's good to have a teammate around to loosen up everyone else. But did people outside of the Ohio State basketball team appreciate Titus's humor? Well, his blog got almost two million hits while he was sitting on the bench, so the answer seems to be "yes."

THE INSTIGATOR

T he problem with stickball is that it does require some
skill. So for little kids and uncoordinated adults, the
Instigator is a good game that nine or more players can play.
But you should have an *odd* number; if you don't, just have a
player sit out and help referee.

The only equipment you need is an object. It can be a ball, a
stuffed animal, or anything else that can be easily lifted.

Pick one player to stand aside. She will be the Instigator, and
she should have a quarter, fifty-cent piece, or dollar coin.
Everyone else is divided into two teams. These two teams
each form a line. Each player on each team should face off
with a player from the opposing team.

Now have everyone sit down. You now have two seated rows
with the players facing each other!

The Instigator places the object (let's say it's a ball) at the
end of the two rows. Then she goes to the other end. She sits
at the opposite end of the object and gives the command:
"Commence stare-down!"

From now on, the rest of the game should be completely quiet,
except for quiet giggling. At this moment, all the players
except for the two closest to the Instigator start staring each

other down. At the same time, all the players hold hands with the players on their left and right. (The first and last players can only hold hands with one person, of course.)

While the players do this, the Instigator keeps the coin concealed in her fist. Then she uncovers the coin so that only the two closest players can see it. (Nobody else is supposed to look! That's why all the other players are staring each other down.)

If the coin is *heads*, each person at the front of their row sees it and squeezes the hand of the person next in line. That person feels the squeeze and passes the squeeze along to the next person in line! Of course, the same thing is happening in the other line, so it's a relay race of reaction times! When the last person in either row feels his hand get squeezed, he jumps up, grabs the object, and runs to the Instigator. (At this point, people may be laughing, cheering, or booing, but that's fine.) Then everyone in that row moves down one spot and the Instigator gets in the front of the row. The kid with the ball is the new Instigator!

Note: You can also play this game with points and/or rewards. The most common problem is a false start when the coin is revealed and it's *tails*, but the first person squeezes someone's hand anyway. Then it's a do-over! If the false start goes all the way down the row and someone grabs the ball when they shouldn't, that team loses one point.

BOERENGOLF = EXCITEMENT!

In Holland, people play a golf game called *Boerengolf* ("farmers' golf"). It works like this: The golfer swings a club that is actually a stick with a wooden shoe attached to it. (Really.) The holes that you try to aim the ball into are actually milk buckets. (Really.) And the ball itself is the size of a miniature soccer ball. (I love this game!)

Best of all, you have to play farmers' golf on a *farm*. No golf carts. You either walk or fire up a tractor! And no wussy obstacles like cute little ponds and sand traps. Instead, golfers have to look out for electric-barbed-wire fences, enraged cows, and enraged cow poop!

Now THAT's a fun sport.

PLAYING WITH SOMEONE'S MIND

If playing with someone's mind is a game, it's probably not a very healthy one! But even so, it IS worth talking about. For instance, imagine this. A friend of yours has a new skateboard. And you say, "Hey, can I look at it for a second?"

Naturally, your friend says no. (Who wouldn't?) But you wheedle and whine, and he finally gives in and rolls the skateboard over to you. You get next to the skateboard and stand on it for one second. Then you get off and give him his skateboard back.

You just blew your friend's mind!

There are lots of other ways to play with someone's mind. When one of your friends comes over to your house, tell him about how you sometimes have conversations with him when he's not actually there. Recount some of the good talks the two of you have had, like this:

"It was really hilarious when you said . . ."

"You won't remember this because you weren't there, but then you answered . . ."

At the end of your little speech, be sure to mention how your friend's *imaginary* self is way more clever than the real person who's there right now! Then casually move on to another topic while your friend stares at you in astonishment.

You can also have fun with the mind of a sleeping person. First, make a "thought" balloon out of a piece of paper. Just take some scissors and cut the edges of the paper so that it looks like the thought balloons you see in comics! Then write something amusing on the thought balloon. Possibilities include:

Girls are purty!

You mess with one bean, you're messing with the whole burrito.

Why do they mock my argyle socks? Why?

User Error: Reboot

While we're on this topic, my brother used to play with my mind all the time. It went a little something like this:

"Bart," he'd say. "Run! The Martians are taking me over with thought-control. They want me to hit you with this big foam noodle!" My brother would then act like he was trying to fight off Martian mind-control even as he went and picked up a big foam noodle.

At this point, I could run or stay put, but it didn't matter. Either way, my brother would start hitting me with a big foam noodle. But the whole time, he'd be saying, "I'm sorry, I'm so sorry. It's the Martians! Try to escape!"

I rarely escaped. For revenge, I would sometimes pretend my brother was invisible. If he said something to me, I would look around as if he weren't there, and then I'd say, "How did you throw your voice like that?" He would insist that he knew I could see him, but I would continue looking around as if there were a hidden loudspeaker broadcasting my brother's words.

"Why can't I see you?" I'd say. "Can you see me?"

At this point, I always saw the same thing: a big foam noodle coming down on me. (Repeatedly!)

FORK FUN!

f you're playing with people's minds, how about this! When you're at a restaurant and finishing up a meal, take two forks and one or two of those little swizzle straws. (You may be able to use a regular straw or even a match for this instead.)

Hold the two forks as shown and wedge the straw between the fork tines. Once you get the straw stuck in there nice and tight, you will

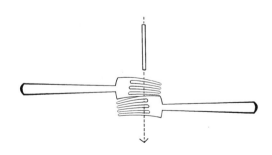

then be able to balance this unwieldy looking thing on your finger! (When you leave, set the forks on the edge of a glass to impress the busboy.)

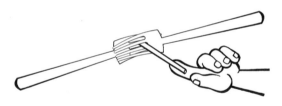

If you do the trick at home and you're using a match, try setting the forks on the edge of the glass and then setting the end of the matchstick on fire. As the fire burns toward the forks, everyone will be on pins and needles waiting for the forks to fall. But they won't, because the fire will go out when it reaches the edge of the glass. (Usually.)

MY, HOW THEY'LL LAUGH!

Go to a racewalking competition. As the contestants go by, point to the leader and shout, "She's walking away with this one!"

PIRATE ATTACK!

Have you ever wondered what it would be like to be a pirate? Of course you have, because those buccaneers are a lot of fun!

But hang on for a second. We have a problem! There are some people who think *ninjas* are cooler than pirates. This is outrageous! I mean, pirates have their own holiday where people imitate them: Talk Like a Pirate Day, on September 19.

So what about it, ninja fans? Sure, you could be copycats and have Talk Like a Ninja Day. But since ninjas are known as *silent* assassins, that would be very silly. On the other hand, I think that having a *Stalk Like a Ninja Day* is a good idea, so let's make it official: June 24 is Stalk Like a Ninja Day!

And now back to the fun guys: pirates! There have been all sorts of pirates throughout history. In ancient times, sea raiders harassed Roman ships. During the Age of Exploration, corsairs attacked Spanish galleons full of gold. And today, pirate meanies in east Africa and Southeast Asia make weekly headlines.

But the most popular image of a pirate is from the "golden age" of piracy between 1600 and 1750. That's when buccaneers like Captain Kidd, Blackbeard, and Captain Morgan sailed the seas. These were the rascals who inspired *Pirates of the Caribbean* and lots of other kooky myths. That's right, *myths!* You see, we know a lot less about pirates than we should.

★ There was at least one pirate named Bart!

Bartholomew (Bart) Roberts stole booty from hundreds of ships. His motto: "A merry life, and a short one." This is quite a coincidence, because that's my motto, too! (Except for the "short" part.) But there is one major difference between us. Bartholomew's pirates declared "war against the whole world," while I have only declared war on Timmy, the little punk down the street who keeps beating me at Wii peewee golf.

PIRATE JOKE!

Why did the pirate *give* no quarter? Because he was too busy *taking* dimes (and gold doubloons)!

★ Pirates had a (twisted) sense of humor.

If pirates attacked a Roman ship, they made sure to treat anyone who was actually Roman very politely. The pirates would apologize and even give the Roman a new, clean toga. Then they would set the Roman free by lowering a ladder over the side of the ship. And if the Roman chose not to climb down the ladder, they threw him overboard.[1]

PIRATES FOR PEACE!

Will Turner: We should turn and fight.
Captain Jack Sparrow: Why fight when you can negotiate?

—*Pirates of the Caribbean: Dead Man's Chest*

---

1. Later pirates would earn a reputation for being much kinder to their captives.

Despite their brawling reputation, most pirates tried to AVOID getting into fights. That's because there was no profit in fighting when you didn't have to. Innocent sailors didn't know that pirates hoped the ships they attacked would just surrender. That's because most of the bloodthirsty sea marauders were actually afraid, too! But pirates WERE sneaky. They knew that getting something for nothing (aka "stealing") was fun, but getting a cannonball shot through your head wasn't. So they would play tricks to get close to other ships:

1. They would fly a friendly flag from their ship.

2. They would conceal their cannons and put lots of chicken coops on the main deck.

3. To hide how fast their ship could go, pirates would often tie barrels to the back of their vessel. Then when they were really close to another ship, they'd cut the barrels loose, giving their ship a "turbo-boost" of speed!

Once they were so close that the other ship couldn't escape, the pirates would strike their friendly flag and fly the Jolly Roger! Its skull-and-crossbones design was designed to strike terror into the hearts of their victims. The idea was that if you surrendered right away, the pirates would be as nice as to you as a pirate could be. But if you fought them, supposedly everyone onboard would be sent to Davey Jones's locker. (Which isn't such a big deal, because Davey forgot the combination to it years ago.)

This clever strategy was so successful, pirate vessels with as few as *five* buccaneers onboard were known to fly the Jolly Roger. So the whole idea behind the Jolly Roger was actually to make peace! Pirate expert Peter T. Leeson says that its real symbol should have been a dove on an olive branch!

★ Pirates were often fair.

In 1719, pirates boarded an English ship off the coast of Africa. When the ship's captain, William Snelgrave, was threatened by the pirates, his sailors cried out, "Don't kill our captain, for there never was a better man." Impressed, a pirate told Snelgrave that his life was safe, since none of his employees complained about him.[2]

★ Pirates believed in equality!

Evidence suggests that the average pirate crew during piracy's "golden age" was about 30 percent black. This was especially impressive, as slavery was legal in most parts of the world at the time. Pirates also elected their own captains.

2. Pirates weren't *always* hung up on money. One of them took Snelgrave's gold watch, jokingly called it a "pretty football," and kicked it overboard.

SURRENDER TO THE BLEEDING HEART!

Besides the skull-and-crossbones depicted on the Jolly Roger, other popular pirate flag designs included a full skeleton, an arm holding a sword, a bleeding heart, and an hourglass. (*"No! The murdering corsairs are flying the hourglass!"*)

★ Pirates loved rules!

Famed pirate leader Captain Morgan and his men wrote a code of ethics that members had to swear by. Soon, other buccaneers started doing the same. Pirates often outlawed thievery (among themselves, that is), gambling, and hard drinking! They even had health insurance. On many pirate ships, if a buccaneer got injured during a raid, he would be paid a set amount, and could expect to be taken care of afterward.

★ Pirates were fun up to the very end.

One buccaneer who had been sentenced to hang said to the onlooking crowd, "I do heartily repent." The crowd hushed. *Wow, this pirate really felt bad for all the plundering he did!*

The pirate then added, "I repent I had not done MORE mischief!"

And everyone cheered!

As you can see, far from being wild, lawless, bloodthirsty nut jobs of the seas, many pirates were actually thoughtful and organized. Heck, even *today's* pirates can make some very good points. Recently, an African pirate said, "We don't consider ourselves sea bandits. We consider sea bandits those who illegally fish . . . and dump waste in our seas."

Here's one last piece of pirate booty. Do you know the song called "What Shall We Do with a Drunken Sailor?" It goes like this:

What shall we do with a drunken sailor
What shall we do with a drunken sailor
What shall we do with a drunken sailor
Early in the morning?

Well, I think that drunken sailor is probably a pirate. I mean, who *else* would pour rum on his Cheerios? Anyway, a guy named Paul Spinrad wondered about this. What would you do with a drunken sailor? Here are a few responses:

"Mark his face with big black markers."
"Swab him down with inadequate sunscreen."
"Make him star in *High School Musical!*"

While these are all very pirate-like ideas, they aren't very nice! I know a better thing to do. How about this:

Turn on cartoons and give him pancakes
Turn on cartoons and give him pancakes
Turn on cartoons and give him pancakes
Early in the morning!

UNEXPECTED FUN

As a fun person, you're constantly "on the go." But climbing trees, sailing around the world, and reading books like this can mean lots of scraped knees and misplaced eyeballs.

Hopefully, all your accidents will be minor, and you'll never have a REAL emergency. Because the only way an emergency can be fun is when it's not a real emergency at all!

For example, I can laugh about it now, but recently I was at another family's house. I went to use the bathroom, but there was a problem. This family had a baby . . . so they had a baby-proof toilet seat! What the heck? I tried and tried, but I could NOT get that stupid seat up.

I thought about ignoring the problem, but I couldn't. You
see, it was an emergency! So I came out of the bathroom and
quietly asked the baby for help. And then that little jerk told
everyone! Oh, the laughter went on and on.

Stupid baby-proof toilet seat!

But one thing I didn't do (though I was tempted!) was call
911. Nearly all nations have emergency numbers, but in
several countries, like England and Scotland, it's 999. When
a Scottish reporter decided to track some recent 999 calls,
he discovered one made by a man who demanded police
action after a car drove through a puddle and soaked him.

"That car got me wet? Emergency!"

Another man called 999 to complain that he got too many onions in his Chinese take-out meal.

"Too many root vegetables? Emergency!"

My favorite was the woman who called 999 because her new rabbit's ears were not floppy enough!

"These ears aren't floppy? Emer—"

Sorry, but, you know, that's just not an emergency.

And finally, a woman in the English city of Manchester called 999 because her cat was playing with a ball of string. I know, that doesn't sound bad, but this cat had been playing with string for TWO HOURS.

Oh, boy.

Let's put a little thought into these phone calls, people! For instance, here's a tricky situation: Imagine you're looking at a live Web cam of a doughnut factory that's a thousand miles away. (Just play along, okay?) Suddenly, you see a worker fall into the doughnut machine, or worse, maybe you see someone steal a maple bar.

Should you call 911 to report the incident? I don't know! But at least we're thinking about it. We can also think about the Boston woman who called 911 because her fourteen-year-old son wouldn't stop playing video games. (Two officers responded and "got the son to obey his mother.")

One of the classic "bad" emergency calls people make is to report a cat stuck in a tree. But those clever 911 operators have learned to give a standard answer to these callers:

"Have you ever seen a dead cat in a tree?"

I've never thought about it that way before![1]

For some reason, many of the silliest 911 calls are related to complaints about fast food. Here are my top three favorites:

3. A Florida man called 911 from the drive-through of a Burger King. Why? He had to *wait* for his lemonade.

---

1. In other words, no cat has ever starved to death from being "stuck" in a tree. When it wants to come down, it'll come down!

2. Another Florida man called 911 *twice* when his Subway sandwiches weren't made the way he wanted them. (His quote: "I got a situation here.")

1. A woman from Florida called 911 *three times* because the McDonald's she was at had run out of McNuggets. Her quote: "This IS an emergency. If I would have known they didn't have McNuggets, I wouldn't have given my money!"

Well, so far I have learned two things about emergencies. First, bad customer service is not a good reason to call 911.

THAT WILL BE XII DOLLARS, PLEASE.

The idea of "fast food" goes all the way back to the ancient Romans. Roadside inns delivered food-to-go to travelers. Archaeologists have nicknamed one of the diners they dug out as "Big Maximus"!

And second, people in Florida need to think harder about their fast food.

I have had a couple of close calls with actual emergencies. My scariest one was when I was hiking on a trail with some kids. Going up the trail, I almost stepped on a rattlesnake. It was really big! I thought about calling 911, but then I realized how dopey that would be, so instead I stepped away from the rattlesnake.

The rattlesnake just sat there.

(Wait, do snakes sit? They don't exactly have butts. Okay, the rattlesnake just remained coiled there.)

I raised my arms and yelled, "Aaaargh!"

"Uh, that's what you do when there's a mountain lion," said a girl named Samantha.

"Got it," I replied. Reaching into my backpack, I got out the perfect thing for the situation. I pulled it over my head and then took a step toward the rattlesnake.

"Is that a mongoose mask?" Samantha asked.

"Yep," I replied. "The natural enemy of the rattlesnake!"

The rattlesnake just remained coiled there.

"Actually," Samantha said, "the mongoose is the enemy of the cobra. Different snake. Different continent."

"Oh." I took off the mask. "So what do we do?"

Samantha looked at the rattlesnake. It just sat there. "We could just walk around it."

"But then the snake will have WON!" I protested. And then we carefully walked WAY around the snake. (I never did call 911!)

BABYSITTING EMERGENCIES

There are "emergencies" and then there are "EMERGENCIES"! Let's say you're babysitting a five-year-old, and he scrapes his knee. You know he's going to be okay, and you want to distract him from the fact that he's bleeding a little. So keep a red cloth on hand! That way you can talk to him while you're dabbing at his knee and he won't notice the blood.

With really young kids, you can take the "emergency" out of an accident by "boo-boo chucking." Here's how it works: If a wee one falls down and cries, have her "scoop" the boo-boo off and throw it at you.

Then you pretend that the boo-boo just hit you. Yell out, "Not the boo-boo!" and fall down in agony. This usually gets the kid laughing!

Note: Don't hurt yourself when you get hit by the boo-boo. That would be a "boo-boo boo-boo," which can be fatal.

You know, now that I think about it, there are an endless number of ways that kids can get into problem situations. Time to get organized!

Problem: You're taking care of a kid who keeps biting you.
Solution: Be less delicious.

Problem: A troublesome kid demands money in order to behave.
Solution: Charge the parents more and give the kid the increase in your salary.

Problem: You're watching a little kid who's out of control.
Solution: Go out to the car and let the child sit in the driver's seat. He or she will happily bang on the steering wheel. (**Note:** Make sure the keys aren't in the ignition.)

Problem: You want the child to "stay within the lines" of the coloring book.
Solution: Have a border collie watch him.

HOW TO GET A KID TO CONFESS!

Imagine that you're responsible for a group of kids. Maybe your teacher left you in charge of the classroom, or perhaps you're getting paid to babysit. (Worst Case Scenario: Your parents made you babysit the triplets!)

You turn your back for a moment (or an hour), when suddenly there's a huge crash! It looks like someone has broken something priceless. And guess who's going to get the blame? No, not me. I wasn't even there! (Or was I?) No, you're in trouble because you were (drum roll, please) . . . IN CHARGE.

What you need to do before any adults show up is figure out exactly what happened and get a confession if possible. First, you'll want to gather your suspect(s) and quarantine the area. If there is more than one suspect, separate them. Also, be sensitive to any trustworthy witnesses who may have seen the event.

Now, on to the crime scene. You're going to need to make a decision: Will you clean up the scene or leave it exactly as it is? It's all or nothing, so this is important. If you choose to clean up the scene, that means you may be guilty of a cover-up. Your suspects will love this, but don't do it if you think you'll get in trouble. Leaving the scene alone is usually preferable; that way you can give a full report to the authorities with a clean conscience. Plus, who wants to sweep up broken crockery? Not me!

Now you're ready to interview your suspects. Try to say as little as possible during your initial questioning, and be sure to TAKE NOTES. Write down the chain of events that your suspect describes. Once you have done so, read back the story to see if the suspect agrees with it. A guilty child will be stressed by

continued on next page

continued from previous page

this—and he'll be even more stressed when you then ask him to reconstruct the whole event backward! Have the suspect give all the events that happened in reverse order. Innocent people have an easy time doing this. Guilty people (and ones under the age of five) have a really hard time with it.

If you think your suspect is innocent, release him with a thank-you for his cooperation. If you think he's guilty, don't push it; just give your report when the adults show up.

Problem: The kids you're babysitting say that you're no fun. (*Gasp!*)

Solution: Break out the Fun Emergency Kit! You'll need to prepare it beforehand, of course. What to put in it? Well, let me think . . . some candy, a yo-yo, and playing cards, for starters. Oh, and money! What Fun Emergency Kit doesn't have a $5 bill in it?[2]

Problem: You think that the child you're taking care of won't go to the bathroom because she's afraid of the toilet.

Solution: Be sympathetic! Try to remember how scary a toilet can be to a little kid. First, it makes a scary sound when it flushes. Second, it's big and cold. Third, there's always a chance that she could fall *into* the toilet.

Heck, now I'm afraid of it!

Problem: You're in charge of a boy who pees all over the toilet.

2. Still desperate? Try putting an odd object on your head as a pretend hat. For some reason, kids love to see you walking around with a waffle iron on your noggin!

Solution: It helps to give a male something to aim at while peeing. (This is why many urinals have pictures of flies on them.) So try throwing a Cheerio into the toilet before he pees. This will keep his pee stream IN the bowl instead of all over it!

BATHROOM FUN!

Put on a cowboy hat. Go in the bathroom. Leave the door open. Get on the toilet backward. With one hand, wave the hat over your head. Next, yell, "Yee-haw!" and slap your thigh with the other hand. Then leave.

Problem: The parents of the kid you're babysitting expect you to clean up her room before she goes to bed.

Solution: Politely explain to the parents that you don't even clean up your OWN room!

Problem: Despite your warnings, the kid you're watching spins around really fast and then suddenly stops. When he does, his face skids around to the back of his head.

Solution: Wow, I didn't even know that was possible! Just stay calm and have the child spin in the *opposite* direction for the same amount of time. Then tell him to stop. This should move things back to where they belong.

Problem: That kid is grouchy!

Solution: Take a picture of the child's face while she is grimacing. Show the picture to her and challenge her to make an even grumpier face. Show her that picture, too, and before you know it, she'll be laughing and in a good mood again!

Then make her go to bed.

ONE LAST FUN EMERGENCY: YOURS!

Your parents have the best intentions, but sometimes they can be overprotective, which might hurt your chances to have fun. To deal with this issue, your first step is to be responsible. You need to show your parents you're committed to safety. So the next time you sit down to read a book, put on a football helmet. Or wear protective goggles when you brush your teeth! (When asked why you're doing this, try not to smile when you say, "You can never be too careful.")

THE MARVELS OF EXPLORATION

Hey, are you going on a trip anytime soon? Great! But before you leave, you have to steal something.

That sounds wrong, doesn't it? While crime doesn't *usually* pay, this innocent crime will add a little fun to the world. Here's what you're going to do: Get your hands on a small item that a friend or relative owns. This may be something the person keeps in his or her locker or bedroom, but just make sure it's not something the person is going to *need* while you're gone! So a cell phone would be a bad choice, but a knick-knack would be good.

★ Definitions: A lie is bad, but a "white lie" is okay, right? So if you get caught pilfering your item, say, "I'm not a thief! I was just making a small white theft." (On second thought, just don't get caught.)

After "borrowing" that knick-knack, you're going to pull an *Amélie*. What, you've never seen that movie? Well, in *Amélie*, there's a French girl named Amélie (who knew?). And she steals her father's garden gnome.

Like me, you may find gnome-napping to be shocking. But wait, there's more! Amélie works out a deal with a flight attendant, who takes the gnome on a world tour. The flight attendant takes pictures of the gnome in front of famous

landmarks like the Eiffel Tower, the Great Wall of China, and Thor Mountain. And these photos are then mailed to Amélie's dad. Naturally, he finds this all very amazing! After logging thousands of miles, the gnome mysteriously returns home, along with a photo album of his travels!

This provides everyone with a good laugh, and it inspires Amélie's dad to travel. As for the gnome, I'm guessing he was glad to be back!

So, I don't want you to copy Amélie, but copy Amélie. Photographing someone else's [*insert possession here*] in faraway places will be fun. Then, when you return, you need to try to sneak the person's [*insert possession here*] back where you found it! As to the photos, you could print them out or just set up a photo page on a free photo-sharing Web site. Then send your "victim" the link!

CLOSE TO HOME

S O WHERE do you think you'll be going? If you're anything like me (we can only hope!), you like to get a map of the world, point to various places on it, and say, "Someday, I'm going THERE." (I hope you're not choosing spots in the middle of the ocean when you do this.) Set your compass for the tropics, and your course for adventure! Or if that's too much trouble, just get a Slurpee and dream about the cool places you might travel to someday.

Let's start close to home. In the summer, you're probably not too far from a county or state fair . . . or maybe a carnival of some sort! I admit there is one very good reason NOT to go to these things: you might step in a horrible combination of pig poop, cotton candy, gum, and the barf of some kid who rode the Zipper one too many times.

But go anyway! Heck, you can always hose off your shoes. Plus, you might win fabulous prizes from the nice men and women who work at the carnival games. These fast-talking "carnies" may sometimes *seem* a little scary, but they love to deliver goodies to clever people (like you!) who have earned it. Follow these strategies for victory:

Making Baskets: Okay, the odds will be stacked against you. Your ball will be overinflated and the hoop will be smaller than regulation size. This will make it hard to sink a shot! The key is to either shoot a PERFECT bank shot or to arc the ball way up high so that it comes straight down through the hoop. Good luck.

P.S. If you try a game where you throw coins onto glasses, do the same thing. Gently toss the coin up high so that it has a better chance of landing (and staying) where you want it.

Shooting Play Guns: When you're playing a shooting game, the problem is that the sights on the gun are probably way off. (I'm sure this is some kind of accident!) During your first few shots, stay calm and don't expect to hit anything. Instead, try to take careful note of where your shot is *actually* going. Then adjust your next shots accordingly!

Dart Throwing: If you're trying to pop balloons, make sure to throw the darts at balloons that have taken a few shots already. Those balloons have weakened, and will fall prey to a dart hunter such as yourself! (Also, to ensure that the darts have a sharp end, sharpen them with your dart sharpener before throwing.)

Important Fun Tip: I know this sounds crazy, but whatever prize you win, you should INSTANTLY give it away. Won a stuffed animal? Give it to the first little kid you see. Won some sort of odd dish? Present it to the first person you see who looks like an odd dish collector. The joy you will see on the surprised person's face will be way more fun than keeping whatever it is you won!

Really.

TRAVELING TO COLLEGE IS FUN!

A "brass ring" is a symbol for a great prize. You know what's going to be really a really great prize? When you get to go away to college! In addition to leaving home and discovering the thrill of learning to do your own laundry, think about the cool classes you'll get to take!

You see, in college, you get to CHOOSE your classes. And since professors need to attract students, they sometimes juice up the courses they offer. That's why if you go to Pitzer College, you can take a class called "Learning From YouTube"!

Here are some other courses you might be interested in as you pursue your higher education:

"Joy of Garbage" (Santa Clara University)

"Knights, Castles, and Dragons" (Boston College)

"Arguing with Judge Judy: Popular Logic on TV Judge Shows (University of California, Berkeley)

"Underwater Basket Weaving" (Yes, really. University of California, San Diego)

"Philosophy and *Star Trek*" (Georgetown University)

"The Art of Walking" (Centre College)

"The Science of Superheroes" (University of California at Irvine)

"Zombies in Popular Media" (Columbia College, Chicago)

"*The Simpsons* and Philosophy" University of California-Berkeley

"The Economics of Sin, Dinosaur Tracks, Communes, Massacres & Poets" (Middlebury College)

"The Science of Harry Potter" (Frostburg State University)

"Myth and Science Fiction: *Star Wars*, *The Matrix*, and *Lord of the Rings*" (Centre College)

"The Strategy of StarCraft" (University of California, Berkley)

THE KNIGHTS RIDE ROUND AND ROUND

Hey, while you're at the amusement park or fair, see if they have a carousel. (You know, a merry-go-round?) Look at the kids riding around and having fun. Little do they know that the carousel traces its beginnings back to the days when knights had jousting tournaments. See, back in the Middle Ages, tournaments were a common entertainment. One event involved a knight on horseback riding toward a metal ring, and trying to stick his lance right through the ring. If you think this sounds easy, try it sometime while riding your bike. (But don't use a REAL lance—and if you do, don't have your brother hold the ring!)

Later versions of this event involved a knight riding a horse in a *circle* (instead of a straight line) while aiming at the ring. This was called the *carosello*. And that's why old-school carousels today still have brass rings that passing kids try to grab as they ride their horsies round and round!

ROAD TRIP!

Okay, let's say you're in the car and headed somewhere fun. But to really enjoy yourself, it's important that you NOT ask this question: "Are we there yet?"

Furthermore, do NOT sing this song to the tune of "Frère Jacques":

Are we there yet? Are we there yet?
Not far now! Not far now!
How long till we get there? How long till we get there?
Mom, I'm sick. Mom, I'm sick.

★ Special Zombie Version: "Are we dead yet?"

But aside from the Question That Must Not Be Named, there are lots of other activities (like screaming contests!) that you can play in the car. Unfortunately, many of them annoy the driver. And since your life is in the driver's hands, it's probably best to keep things low-key.

Hey, have you heard of sleepovers where blindfolded girls give each other makeovers? This results in kooky mistakes that always get laughs. But taking it one step further, one mom I know lets her daughters give her a makeover on road trips! The mom sits in the front passenger seat and gives her daughters her makeup kit. Then she reclines her chair as far as is safe. Then she closes her eyes while the girls work their magic. Although the girls aren't blindfolded, the car *is* in motion, and their mom's face is upside down!

This has led to some very interesting moments.

Fun Tip: Whenever putting makeup on someone, try to use lipstick to make a "kiss" mouth shape on their forehead, cheek, neck, or anywhere else where you think they may not notice it.

FUN PLACES TO TRAVEL

As you drive along, roadside attractions may pop up on your route. You know the kinds of places I'm talking about: "Is Seeing Believing? Visit the Gopher Mound of Mystery!" Although these attractions might sound fun when you're bored, I find that they often make me sad. ("Hey . . . This is a MOLE-hill!")

But there are some roadside attractions that ARE worth stopping for! First up is the **Kennedy Space Center in Merritt Island, Florida.** Among other things, it has the world's fourth-largest building! I still think of this as one of the best road trips in my life (and I've been on three so far!).

A slightly less educational trip would be to the **Mud Hole Belly Flop Competition in Dublin, Georgia.** (**Warning:** It's held at the Summer Redneck Games.) How do you win this competition? You guessed it—you jump into a mud hole and try to splash up as much mud as possible. (My inside sources tell me that to achieve maximum splash, you should do a scissors jump.[1])

West Virginia's Road Kill Cook-Off is held each autumn. It's a good place to taste squirrel-gravy biscuits, and if you're lucky, you can meet the Road Kill Queen! (Really.) And over in Crosville, Tennessee, is the world's biggest tree house . . . although

a house that uses SEVEN trees for support should really be called a "*trees* house"! Called the **Minister's Tree House,** it's five stories tall and growing.

---

1. After jumping, wrap both hands around one knee and bring it up to your waist. Keep the other leg straight while falling slightly backward into the water.

There are tons of awesome museums in Washington, D.C., but the best one might be the **National Air and Space Museum.** It has almost every great artifact of flight you can think of. Want to see the Wright brothers' original 1903 plane? It's there, as is the *Spirit of St. Louis*, the *Apollo 11* command module, and the Intergalactic Hyperspace Drone.[2] While you're there, catch a shuttle to the museum's other branch, the Udvar-Hazy Center.

The Sagan Planet Walk in Ithaca, New York, is probably the best way there is to understand our tiny corner of the universe. You take a tour that starts in downtown Ithaca, and puts you in a scale model of the Solar System. Not only do you get a passport to the Solar System, but you can also see how far the planets are from the sun (and each other). The walk is less than a mile, and if you get your passport stamped at all the planets, you can get free admission at the museum called the Sciencenter. (Fun fact: Using the same scale, if you wanted to understand the distance from our Solar System to the nearest star, you'd have to hoof it from New York to Hawaii!)

Do you like submarines? Who doesn't! If you get a chance, dive over to the **Submarine Force Museum in Groton, Connecticut.** (Sorry.) There are lots of exhibits and replicas, and you can go onboard the world's first nuclear submarine, the *Nautilus*. Ooh, and if you prefer flying

2. Oops, that's apparently on a mission right now.

squash, head south to Delaware, where the annual **Punkin Chunkin** competition is held. It's the greatest pumpkin-launching event in the world. When you set up to watch, give yourself some room . . . those catapults and trebuchets can chuck pumpkins over three thousand feet!

Up in Toronto, they have a cool four-day festival called **Buskerfest.** This is a great chance to see break dancers, stilt walkers, fire eaters, acrobats, singers, mimes, magicians, and jugglers in their native habitat: the *street!* Just by walking around, you can see more entertainment in one day than most people do in six months. (Not counting the times they were reading this book.)

The House on the Rock (Spring Green, Wisconsin) is tough to describe. How about "a truly bizarre combination of buildings and items"? If you've been to the **Winchester Mystery House** (San Jose, California), you know what I mean. (And if you haven't been there, go to the Winchester Mystery House!)

If you like setting off rockets, consider the **Titan Missile Museum in Sahuarita, Arizona.** It includes an underground missile silo—with a missile still IN the silo! As part of the tour, you get to go to the underground control room for a launch. (It's simulated.) In addition to learning some rocket science, you will also get a good reminder about the greatest threat to fun the world faces: missile silos that *aren't* simulated!

If you find yourself in Portland, Oregon, see if you can't take the short trip to the **Evergreen Aviation & Space Museum in McMinnville.** Among other things, it has the world's largest plane ever built: the *Spruce Goose*. The first time I saw it, I couldn't believe it was real, and not something cooked up by a special- effects team!

If you're driving through Seattle, take time to see the giant troll living under the north end of the **Aurora Bridge.** Known as the Fremont Troll, it's easy to find; just go to the troll's Twitter page for more information. (Really.)

Finally, see if you can find time to go visit the **Grand Coulee Dam in Washington.** It's big. How big? The dam is the biggest hydroelectric station on the continent. Best of all, it has a glass elevator that goes down the face of the dam. *Yikes!*

TRAVELING ABROAD

Most of the countries in the world are fascinating places, and you should go to as many of them as possible. However, since you could go almost *anywhere* and have a great time, let me narrow things down and tell you that if you're looking for FUN, here are . . .

Six Places Not to Go!

6. **The Loneliest Road in America,** also known as US Route 50, runs from California to Maryland. The stretch of the road that runs through Nevada is so horrible and barren, drivers are warned to stay away unless they are survivalists. There are only five towns along this entire section, which goes for more than three hundred miles. Anyone who stops in all five towns gets a survival certificate signed by the governor of Nevada! (Seriously.)

5. In Canada is a mountain that is actually quite beautiful. Just don't try to climb it. That's because **Mount Thor** (on Baffin Island) has the greatest sheer vertical drop in the world.

4. Stinky cities are not fun! So avoid **Rotorua, New Zealand.** It's known as the most noxious city on the planet. (Volcanic fumes are responsible.) And **Cairo, Egypt,** has the "stinkiest" air of any city—but its smelly problems are all man-made!

3. When a place is called the **Gate of Hell,** you already know to keep your distance. And in Turkmenistan is just such a place! See, back in 1971, a drilling rig dug into a gigantic underground cavern. Poisonous, flammable gases started coming out of it. So someone set the whole thing on fire! And a colossal inferno has been burning there EVER SINCE.

2. The **Zilov Gap** in Russia is four hundred miles of roadless wilderness. That actually sounds pretty interesting, except that the wilderness can get so muddy, it takes an hour just to slog the length of a football field. Forget that! (And if you choose to fly over the Zilov Gap, steer clear of the Mir Diamond Mine. It's a hole that is so colossal, it has its own air flow, and has been known to suck helicopters into it!)

1. It's a little hard to explain where **Bir Tawal** is, because it's just a crummy chunk of hot sand and rocks in the Middle East that nobody wants. Neither Egypt nor Sudan will take it, so let's just say that it's known as the "Most Undesired Spot on Earth." (And that includes Antarctica!)

FUN: An Endangered Species?

Just as there can be no light without dark, fun cannot exist without . . . un-fun. It's shocking, but there are times when fun can be weakened and even destroyed! That means it is super-important for us to identify un-fun things so that we can resolve or avoid them. So pay attention to these useful examples!

Un-Fun Situation: It's breakfast time and you only have those tiny boxes of cereal that have, like, seven cereal flakes in them.

The Fun Way Out: Open forty of the little boxes. (Then make toast!)

Un-Fun Situation: You have a normal-size cereal box. *Yes!* But now you can't figure out how to put together the free toy that came in it.

The Fun Way Out: Give the unassembled toy as a "gift" to a young child. Then take notes as she puts it together.

Un-Fun Situation: A friend congratulates you for winning a tough game of Wii badminton by dumping an ice-chest of Gatorade over your head.

The Fun Way Out: Impress onlookers by calmly putting a Gatorade-covered finger in your mouth and saying, "Mmmm . . . orangey."

Un-Fun Situation: While hanging out at the beach, you see a group of overweight people enthusiastically playing volleyball.

The Fun Way Out: I'm sorry. I just pictured this and I'm at a loss for words.

THE MOST UN-FUN THING OF ALL

What is the most un-fun thing you can think of? I don't know about you, but for me, what's REALLY un-fun is when my relatives embarrass me. Here are some of the ways they have done this:

★ My dad makes me hold his hand in the mall. (This really sucks in the food court.)

★ My sister likes to tell strangers about the time I peed in front of everyone. (Look, it was a crowded swimming pool, okay?)

★ I stopped to fill up the car with gas while driving with my mom. Oops! I spilled gas on my shoes. When the attendant came by, my mom pointed at me and said, "If you smell any gas, it's coming from him."

Then they both laughed really hard.

Then I blushed, which wasn't helpful. You see, maybe the worst thing about being embarrassed is when everyone KNOWS you're embarrassed! But unless you move to another planet or dimension, being embarrassed by relatives is one kind of un-fun we just have to live with.

And maybe that's not so bad. After all, despite the un-fun, there are LOTS of cool things about having brothers, sisters, and second cousins whose names you can't remember . . . and I'm sure I'll think of some in a minute! In the meantime, let's keep looking at ways to salvage fun from un-fun situations!

Problem: You're video conferencing with someone when you lean back and fall off your chair.

Salvage Operation: Yell, "The connection's down!" and then log off.

Problem: You forgot your best friend's birthday.

Salvage Operation: Get a good gift. And a card. Write in the card something like, "You thought that I forgot your birthday . . . but I was actually out *celebrating* it!" Then give the card to your friend and see if it works. (Good luck.)

Problem: You just ran into a glass door. Why? You thought it was open.

Salvage Operation: Since your hands (and maybe your face) are already planted on the glass, start moving your palms around on the glass like a mime. By pretending you're a mime, you'll fool people into thinking that you're way cooler than a dork who runs into glass doors![1]

Problem: Your room is a total mess. You're actually not that embarrassed about it, but you're going to get into BIG trouble when your parents see it.

Salvage Operation: Put a note on your door: "Has anyone seen my room? I can't find it." Your parents will be

---

1. I accidentally walked through a screen door once. This is more embarrassing than walking into a glass door, since you can actually SEE a screen door. (I wasn't hurt, but I did strain myself a little.)

so amused, you'll have a short grace period to clean it up before getting in trouble.

Un-Fun Situation: You bend over to pick up a pencil in the school hallway and the twenty-sided dice you keep in your shirt pocket spill out everywhere.
Salvage Operation: Hold your arms up and shout, "We've got a situation here!" Then wave people back like there's been a toxic spill and gather up your dice.

Un-Fun Situation: You haven't sucked on a pacifier in a LONG time. (Like me.) But you still sometimes wake up to find your thumb in your mouth. (Like me!) And this would be VERY embarrassing if someone found out.
Salvage Operation: Just before going to bed, remove both of your thumbs and put them in a glass on the nightstand.

Un-Fun Situation: You come up to a shop door and pull and pull on it. It won't budge! But the sign says they're open! Then you notice another sign. It says, "Push."
Salvage Operation: Option 1. Bend down and pretend to tighten your shoelaces. Then pat your pockets and look surprised, as if you've just realized you have no money. Then casually walk off. Option 2. Run away immediately. Never return to that place again.

THE WORLD'S MOST UN-FUN PHRASE!

I've done a lot of research to find out what sentence can sink fun faster than a bowling ball dropped in the kiddie pool. It turns out that if you ask a question using the word "moist" (as in, "How did these potato chips get moist?"), you'll put a damper on any event!

BRINGING IT ALL BACK HOME

You know, I just had an insight. It's possible for a thing to be so incredibly and horribly un-fun, it comes all the way around and becomes the MOST FUN THING EVER. You know, like this book! I know it sounds crazy, but trust me. I may not be wiser than you, but I'm definitely older. (In fact, I think I just tripped over your umbilical cord!) To prove my point that horrible un-fun can become jaw-droppingly "regular" fun, here's a good example:

A TV show once decided to help a couple celebrate their fiftieth wedding anniversary. So the show hired a party planner to put together the *perfect* event. Things went well until there was one little problem. All the party guests were handed sparklers to wave around as the band played a song and the happy couple danced.

And at this incredibly touching moment, rose petals were dropped from the ceiling. Romantic! But the problem was that the rose petals were fake—and flammable. So TV viewers saw a lovely party suddenly turn into a disaster zone as fires broke out, people screamed, and stagehands rushed in spraying fire extinguishers!

Meanwhile, the band kept playing its song: "I Can't Smile Without You."

Since nobody was actually hurt, this was awesome! In fact, it may have been the most fantastically un-fun fun moment in the history of fun. You know everyone at that event talked about it for the rest of their lives! And as the smoke cleared from the party decorations, I understood that the flaming rose-petal party had an important lesson for all of us: Just when we think things can't get any worse, they just might turn out to be pretty fun!

And so I command you: Close this book, go forth, and HAVE SOME FUN.

Or take a nap. (Either one!)

ACKNOWLEDGMENTS

You know what would be *really* fun? Taking all the credit for this book myself! Unfortunately, my wife, Lynn, says I can't. So I'll thank her first, for making sure that I behave in a way that is fun AND fair!

I would also like to thank Brody vanderSommen, Aaron Judd, Lee Wassink, Dave and Caleb Sohigian, Christie Nicholson, Charlene Marshall, Troy Taylor, Larry Smith, Sean Mackin, Windell H. Oskay, Virginia Wassink, Benjamin Golliver, Sheila King, Tom Booth, Carol Guttzeit, Kathy Logan, Austin Sharp, Parker Stevenson, Adam Cadien, Karen Kroner Amstutz, Mariam Kanso, Paul Spinrad, all the Grows, Mary King, Mr. Cuddles, Jon Cadien, Janice Johnson, Jennifer King, Jared Smith, and Suzanne Taylor.

The six-word memoirs in the Wild Words chapter come from SMITH Teens (smithteens.com), which is a project of the storytelling community *SMITH Magazine*.

Oh, and a VERY special thank-you to anybody who stopped by www.bartking.net to contribute a good joke . . . or a bad one!

SELECT BIBLIOGRAPHY

Atlas Obscura. http://atlasobscura.com.

Barksdale, Nick. "You Had Me at Hello." Cardus.ca, November 20, 2009.

Birkbeck, Matt. "Allentown man butts in on judge at sentencing." *Morning Call*, October 2, 2009. http://articles.mccall.com/2009-10-02/news/4451255_1_bledsoe -stengel-robbery.

Blount, Roy Jr. *Alphabet Juice*. New York: Farrar, Straus & Giroux, 2008.

Burau, Caroline. *Answering 911: Life in the Hot Seat*. Minnesota: Borealis Books, 2007.

Cathcart, Thomas, and Daniel Klein. *Heidegger and a Hippo Walk Through the Pearly Gates*. New York: Viking, 2009.

Crain, Caleb. "Bootylicious." *New Yorker*, September 7, 2009.

Egan, Mark. "'Proud non-reader' rapper Kanye West turns author." Reuters, May 26, 2009. http://www.reuters.com/article/idUSTRES4P5L820090526.

Encyclopedia of Immaturity. Palo Alto, CA: Klutz, 2007.

"Englishman's metal detector finds record treasure trove." CNN.com, September 24, 2009. http://www.cnn.com/2009/WORLD/Europe/09/24/staffordshire .uk.gold.hoard/.

Evil Mad Scientist Laboratories. http://www.evilmadscientist.com.

Foundation for Fair Civil Justice. http://www.legalreforminthenews.com.

Gordon, Whitson. "Use a Glass as a Smartphone Sound Booster." Lifehacker.com, January 8, 2010. http://www.lifehacker.com.au/2010/01/from-the-tips-box -smartphone-speakers-wallet-holes-fire/.

Graham-Cunning, John. *The Geek Atlas*. Sebastopol, CA: O'Reilly Media, 2009.

Hafner, Katie. "Driven to Distraction, Some Unfriend Facebook." *New York Times*, December 21, 2009.

Hopkin, Karen. "Babies Already Have an Accent." *Scientific American*, November 6, 2009.

Instructables: One of the Coolest Websites Ever. http://www.instructables.com.

It Made My Day: Little Moments of WIN. http://itmademyday.com.

Klosterman, Chuck. *Eating the Dinosaur*. New York: Scribner, 2009.

Leibovich, Mark. "Every Dog (and Norseman) Has His Day." *New York Times*, October 11, 2009.

Liew, Jonathan. "Moneyfacing: The Web's latest craze." *Telegraph*, December 8, 2009. http://www.telegraph.co.uk/news/newstopics/howaboutthat/6761157 /Moneyfacing-the-webs-latest-craze.html.

SELECT BIBLIOGRAPHY

McGovern, Una. *Lost Crafts: Rediscovering Traditional Skills*. Edinburgh: Chambers, 2008.

Moskowitz, Clara. "Smiles Predict Marriage Success." LiveScience.com, April 14, 2009. http://www.livescience.com/culture/090414-smile-marriage.html.

National Toy Hall of Fame. http://www.museumofplay.org/.

Netter, Sarah. "When 911 Emergencies Are Not So Much." ABC News, March 10, 2009. http://abcnews.go.com/US/story?id=7039456&page=1.

Nicholson, Christie. "It's Funny Because It's True." *Scientific American*, October 13, 2009.

NotMartha.org. "Meat Hand." October 27, 2009. http://www.notmartha.org/archives/2009/10/27/meat-hand/.

O'Mara, Lesley. *Laughable Latin*. London: Michael O'Mara, 2004.

Orth, Stephan. "Summer Fun, Teutonic Style." *Der Spiegel*, August 14, 2009.

Ostler, Nicholas. *Ad Infinitum: A Biography of Latin*. New York: Walker & Company, 2007.

"Pan con Tomate." Saveur.com. http://www.saveur.com/article/Kitchen/Pan-Con-Tomate.

Powell, Padgett. *The Interrogative Mood: A Novel?* New York: Ecco, 2009.

Sample, Ian. "Christmas card snowflakes 'corrupt nature' by defying laws of physics." Guardian.co.uk, December 23, 2009. http://www.guardian.co.uk/science/2009/dec/23/christmas-card-snowflakes-nature-physics.

Sandel, Michael J. *Justice: What's the Right Thing to Do?* New York: Farrar, Straus & Giroux, 2009.

Schworm, Peter. "Colleges find juicy titles swell enrollment." *Boston Globe*, October 15, 2009.

Spinrad, Paul. "What Shall We Do With a Drunken Sailor?" Boingboing.net, December 2, 2009. http://boingboing.net/2009/12/02/what-shall-we-do-wit-1.html.

Squires, Nick. "'His Tremendousness' dies at, aged 73." *Telegraph*, November 25, 2009.

Thamel, Pete. "A Last Man Off the Bench Rides a Blog to Stardom." *New York Times*, December 26, 2009.

"Training a Flip-Flop Army." *Morning Edition*, National Public Radio, September 15, 2009.

Valdesolo, Piercarlo. "Flattery Will Get You Far." *Scientific American*, January 12, 2010. http://www.scientificamerican.com/article.cfm?id=flattery-will-get-you-far.

"William Kidd." *Encyclopedia of World Biography Supplement*, Vol. 21. Gale Group, 2001. Reproduced in Biography Resource Center. Farmington Hills, MI: Gale, 2009.